PEOPLE STUFF

PEOPLE STUFF

BEYOND PERSONALITY PROBLEMS
An Advanced Handbook for Leadership

ZOË ROUTH

First published by Inner Compass Australia in July 2020
Reprinted January 2023
This edition July 2024

Copyright © Zoë Routh 2020, 2021, 2023, 2024

Zoë Routh asserts the moral right to be identified as the author of *People Stuff* and all associated products.

ISBN 978-0-9944119-9-0 Paperback
ISBN 978-0-6488773-4-9 Amazon POD
ISBN 978-0-9944119-9-0 IngramSpark POD
ISBN 978-0-6488773-0-1 Epub ebook
ISBN 978-0-6488773-1-8 Kindle ebook

Subjects: Leadership, Workplace Culture, Management, Human Resources & Personnel Management

All rights reserved. Except as permitted under the Australian Copyright Act 1968 (for example, a fair dealing for the purposes of study, research, criticism or review), no part of this publication may be reproduced, stored in a retrieval system, communicated or transmitted in any form or by any means, mechanical, electronic, photocopying, recording or otherwise, without the prior written permission of the Publisher.

Cover art and all illustrations by Lynne Cazaly – lynnecazaly.com
Author photograph by Paul Chapman – modeimagery.com.au
Typesetting, book design and printing – exlibris.com.au

For more information about the author
Zoë Routh
Email: zoe@zoerouth.com
www.zoerouth.com

Disclaimer
This book is intended to give general information only. The material herein does not represent professional advice. The author expressly disclaims all liability to any person arising directly or indirectly from the use of, or for any errors or omissions, the information in this book. The adoption and application of the information in this book is at the reader's discretion and is his or her sole responsibility.

The real voyage of discovery
consists not in seeking new lands,
but in seeing with new eyes.

Marcel Proust

PRAISE FOR *PEOPLE STUFF*

"Leadership is a daily rollercoaster ride. When leading people, often the only thing we can control is ourselves ... the way we react and the way we respond. People Stuff is an insightful and practical guide for any leader. It's a must-read book to help you lead with wisdom when it comes to all that 'people stuff.'"
Gabrielle Dolan, bestselling author of
Real Communication and Stories for Work

"People Stuff goes beyond leadership styles, tactics and tips, to the very core of how you see yourself, your people and your organisation. This is an advanced book about developing wisdom and mastery as a leader. Essential reading for any leader who wants to be the best version of themselves."
Peter Cook, Chairman, Thought Leaders Business School

"Zoë turns complex information into practical stories that we can relate to and apply for ourselves to make us better leaders."
Andrew Spencer, Chair, Australian Farm Institute

"If understanding people in depth – from self to others – is a meta-skill for leaders in 2020 and beyond, then People Stuff is a guiding light on becoming better at this for leaders at all stages."
Matt Linnegar, CEO, Australian Rural Leadership Foundation

"People Stuff is a great read. It is a practical and insightful guide for leaders who want to fine-tune their leadership when it comes to their people, while keeping it real."
Sharon Tuffin, CEO, Karralika Programs Inc.

"People Stuff is insightful, practical and of enormous value in addressing the real issues that impact everyday business. What I loved about this book was that it helped me think more deeply about these everyday issues and then develop better approaches and solutions to these issues."
Dr Ian Taylor, Executive Director,
Cotton Research and Development Corporation

"Filled with wise insights, penetrating (and useful) questions, and a brilliant set of archetypes, People Stuff made me reconsider what leadership is, and how to do it well. I would highly recommend you partake of Zoë's practical wisdom, as it will help you be a better version of the leader you are."
Andrew Deering, Leader in People and Operations,
Author, Coach, Facilitator, The Deering Group

For Us

Contents

Introduction xv

Part one: Context

The start of gaining perspective 1

The problems you face as a leader 3

Leadership in crisis 5

Developmental frameworks for *People Stuff* 8

Together we'll create the solution 9

How to use *People Stuff* 10

Part two: The practice of perspective

Checking in 13

The practice of perspective 17

Your leadership navigation tool: The practice of perspective map 19

1. Let's start with expand: sense-making 20

2. Next, it's time to Focus: We need to make sense 32

3. Mastering thoughts, or the art of being sensible and wise 39

4. Mastering feelings, or the art of being sensitive and compassionate 43

What affects our perspective 45

Other factors that affect our perspective 50

Part three: YOU

Perspective on self 53

About archetypes 57

About shadow work 59

The five archetypes 62

Archetype 1: The Elder 62

Archetype 2: The Warrior 72

Archetype 3: The Diplomat	81
Archetype 4: The Guardian	90
Archetype 5: The Pioneer	99

Part four: THEM

Perspective on others	109
The turbulent Four Devils	113
The Four Devils	123
Devil 1: The Firebug	124
Devil 2: The Storm Driver	128
Devil 3: The Ground Splitter	132
Devil 4: The Water Bomber	137
Developing emotional competency in self and others	141
How to develop the skills of being real (in ourselves and others)	142

Part five: US

Perspective on the bigger things	151
Make a Declaration	156

Conclusion — 159

Q & A — 163

Resources for leaders — 171

Gratitude and Acknowledgments — 177

About the Author — 179

Appendices

Appendix A: Trust in public life	181
Appendix B: Famous thoughts on wisdom, compassion and perspective	183

Figures in the text

Figure 1: Model of the practice of perspective	19
Figure 2: The dynamics in the system of the Happy Pants Company	29
Figure 3: Sample scenario planning	33
Figure 4: Problem tree for Frank and Karen	35
Figure 5: The five archetypes	57
Figure 6: Shadows of the five main archetypes	61
Figure 7: The Four Devils	114

INTRODUCTION

We live in extraordinary times. Dickens might say: it was the best of times, it was the King Kong craziest of times! We have the world's knowledge in our pocket. We can geo-locate simultaneously across four continents with the power of videoconferencing. We can grow replacement body parts in a lab. We can print pizza. Mind blowing.

This interconnected world offers a cornucopia of cultures, tastes, and adventures. We don't even need to leave our living rooms for these experiences; virtual reality gives us a banquet of sights and sounds. All this connection means that we can evolve as a species at light speed. We can share resources instantaneously and build ideas exponentially. It's the compounding effect on steroids! No longer do we look for Moon shots, but Mars shots![1] This is the first generation in human history that is likely to become an interplanetary civilisation.

This magical world comes with some risks. We are blind to the ramifications – while our systems are amazing, they're not resilient. A breakdown pulls a thread that unravels entire global networks. Thresholds can be breached quickly, threatening total system breakdowns.

When the internet crashes, entire businesses are paralysed. No emails, no research, no surfing. Without checking phones or devices we are forced into that archaic practice known to ancestors as 'in-person conversation'.

---

1 It used to be that 'shooting for the moon' captured the human imagination for anything is possible. Now we have nations and leaders vying for human-led expeditions to Mars. The Moon is just too close now!

Things can get serious fast. Social media can spread rumours and innuendo around the globe in an instant. When this is nothing more than speculation about the latest celebrity meltdown or alien abduction, then it's nothing more than titillation. When it's a margin call of the highly interconnected USA financial system (such as the Global Financial Crisis of 2008), the fallout is global. The recession was felt around the world for years. As I write this book, the COVID-19 crisis is in full swing, spreading around the planet, and the future of global health unknown. Millions infected, hundreds of thousands dying, healthcare systems busting at the seams, and millions out of work.

If ever we needed solid leadership, then it's now. The complexity and scale of this pandemic requires nimble and collaborative efforts.

Amid this transformation, we are experiencing a crisis of trust in leadership. We have lost faith in our political leaders. We have lost faith in our religious and business leaders. In our media. And for some, the very idea of democracy. From endless Royal Commissions to leadership spills, from fake news, to cyber hacking and even to the weird worship of social influencers. As a collective, we've lost our perspective.

Given our current context, we simply cannot lead the way that we used to. We need to turn leadership on its head. Whether leading on a global stage or a local one, leadership needs a new point of view. A new perspective to help us see more clearly.

This book is for you

You're a leader, contending with these crazy times and trying to do your best. You're sitting in your office, staring out the window. Your vision is clear and compelling. Your passion and energy is boundless. You feel capable and competent. When things are going well, you love your team and enjoy the keen dynamic. But today has been a tough day. The pressure to deliver is immense, the scrutiny relentless – both inside the organisation and outside of it. The world seems to be going to hell in a hand basket, and you're left holding the handles.

And there's this other stuff. The 'people stuff'.

It's been a day of interruptions. Complaints. Of closed door, hushed conversations with overtones. Staff at each other's throats. Or worse, quietly seething. There are constant small frictions. It's the little things in the people stuff that burn you, just a bit, each day. At this point your inner voice kicks in: "Why are they so difficult? I'd love to sack them all and start again. If it weren't for people, leadership would be so much easier."

People stuff gets people down. It's frustrating and exhausting. Leadership is not a solo activity and teamwork is just that – work. While people can be the biggest source of headaches at work, they can also be the biggest joy. Together we can wrestle challenges to the ground, kick spectacular goals, and celebrate triumphant, happy in each other's company.

Let's do more of that – the fun stuff in people stuff.

Let's face it, there are an infinite number of books about leadership to help you through. From authentic to transformational, ethical and collaborative ... these focus on the many different *styles* of leadership you can adopt.

In *People Stuff*, we will create a lens for how you will *see*.

As leaders, we need to shift how we see the world, others, and ourselves. An advanced handbook for creating this seismic shift, *People Stuff* looks at perspective as the catalyst for all change. If we change how we see, we change how we behave as a result. When we change the way we look at things, things don't change, *we* do. And we want this to be a positive and powerful experience for us and those around us.

At the heart of it, we need to master complexity and master inclusion. The more we see, the farther we look, the more we include in our perspective. And the more responsive and informed we will be as leaders. We can take smart action after that.

People Stuff is about developing wisdom and the ability to master leadership in complexity. It is about developing compassion and the ability to master inclusion as a practice with no limits. And about developing people and the ability to show up, centred and composed.

People Stuff is for leaders who deal with people every day. You might have a team you manage, or run an organisation with several teams in play. Regardless of the scale and scope of your leadership context, this book helps with the people stuff you face. The health of every organisation depends on it. People stuff skills keep your people and your business units thriving and interacting with others.

In *Loyalty* (2018), I reflected on organisational culture and the need to adapt to the pace of world change, and the far-reaching influence of automation and globalisation. But in 2020 the pace and scale of change has cranked up to a whole new level. Regardless of our context or what's happening around us, the real stuff – the people stuff – is our ongoing work.

I am now into my fourth decade of working with leaders around the globe. In this time, I have mapped many patterns of individual and team behaviour – some that work, some that don't. I've been an insider to some of the most challenging experiences of leadership: mutinies, sackings, board spills, infidelities, betrayals, bitchiness and bullying, meltdowns, financial implosions, backroom politics, undermining, white anting, and toxic cultures. My first priority was to support the leader and their team through the crisis. Then it was to unpack what happened. I always wondered: 'How did we get here'? How do good people with good intentions end up in such torn and difficult circumstances? What causes the chaffing and needling? The bitterness and frustration? Is it possible to build a workplace where these things fade away? Where work gets done, people love what they do and who they do it with?

My musings kept me digging and exploring. I wanted to find out what was behind people's drivers. Where leaders should start in dealing with the people stuff, and how to show up more composed. How can we become the better version of ourselves?

As a seeker, I ferreted insights from books and other leaders. I stumbled on insights in my own observations and reflection. I gained new awareness when courageous people cared enough to tell me how my behaviour affected them. Those were the toughest: like being told you've been tracking dog poo across the floor when returning from a walk. Mortification, embarrassment. And a need to clean things up.

One of my deeply-held beliefs is that who we are and how we show up ripples across the world. Interconnectivity is not just for the internet, it's for our collective consciousness. As I drilled into the immediate and painful experiences of leaders, I also shared their deep concern for the future of the planet and humanity. But when zooming out, there is a danger we become paralysed in the face of the complexity and scale of the issues. This concerned me. If we are to make progress against any challenges, then we need to galvanise our creativity and collaborate to find solutions. Paralysis is not an option. How then can we see the big picture, understand it, and then take action in our own sphere of influence in a meaningful way? I became obsessed with helping big thinkers, with big hearts, to make a big difference.

Zooming in and zooming out became a way of seeing and being for me. I learned to flow from the big picture and bring it back to immediate actions and what I could do as an individual leader. This is my focus with leaders now. We work on deep personal awareness, broad global awareness, and practical steps to work our way forward through it together. I developed maps for understanding the territories: a map for ourselves as leaders, a map for understanding others, and a map for understanding the big picture.

The little things that drive us nuts in the people stuff are critical. The 'little things' are things that clog our productivity engine. Little bits of friction that wear down at the joins, bit by bit. The little things affect the whole. It's in dealing with these little things that we look after the big things. In this book, we will zoom out to the big picture and then zoom back in again to the practical aspect of dealing with the immediate and painful people stuff bits.

Zooming in and out, leading with wisdom and compassion, are the skills I wish to leave you with. In doing so, one leader at a time, we make the world a better place.

Zoë Routh
Canberra, Australia
June 2020

PART ONE

Context

The start of gaining perspective

It's happened more than once. There's a triangular patch of dirt at the top of our driveway that from my perspective, gives space for misaligned reversals up the steep slope. From a dog's perspective, it's also the perfect spot, apparently, to do its business. On a few occasions we've been left a nice pile of steaming turds. In my mind's eye I imagine the dog doing its work and then carrying on, satisfied. I imagine the owners looking furtively around for witnesses, then shuffling away – having made the escape – leaving the mess for someone else to deal with.

How then can someone blatantly ignore the rules of both dog ownership and neighbourly courtesy?

People can drive you nuts. It's the small things … that go on, day after day.

The public space smokers. The public transport loud-talking mobile phone users. The hog-the-whole sidewalk slow walkers. At work, there are the gossipers. The underminers. The accountability-shirkers. The "it's not my job" bleaters. The "they don't pay me enough" complainers.

It's enough to drive us mad! How can people lack so much self-awareness? How can people be so damned inconsiderate and selfish?

We could aim to rise above it. If someone cuts us off in traffic, take a deep breath, pause, and ask: "Just like me, this person might be having a bad day." Find a modicum of compassion, resist the urge to ram their tailgate or flip them a rude gesture, and let them through.

I try to think of this as I stare at yet another pile of dog shit on my lawn. Wisdom and compassion. Breathe (gag). Pause. Is the dog owner just having a bad day? Or are they just an inconsiderate jerk?

It's possible they had more issues than they were equipped to deal with. It's possible that their life had been a series of tragedies and misfortune so that their default response was aggression and defensiveness. Or maybe they just forgot the plastic poop baggie.

We'll never know.

Here we come to the heart of people stuff.

People do and say stuff that drives us crazy. Stuff we find annoying at best, reprehensible at worst. We don't know what's driving their behaviour, but as leaders we have to deal with it.

There are two ways of dealing with this:

1. React

or

2. Respond.

Reacting feels good. There is nothing more satisfying than moral outrage. "I'm right, they're wrong. They're an asshole, I am virtuous".

Responding without an emotional, judgmental narrative takes more work. It takes great emotional agility to get to the point where you can witness someone's poor behaviour and all its consequences, and then address it with grace.

I'm still working on that. My guess is that if you've picked up this book, you are too. The move to be more Zen starts with a shift in perspective.

This perspective is the gateway to change.

If we can see the furtive dog owner as a fellow human with all their beautiful flaws, then we can move to a better leadership response.

Perspective is pivotal. It's central to how we evolve as humans. Perspective is core to making effective short-term interventions as well as long-term plans.

It's not for the faint-hearted. When we see with new eyes, our past beliefs drop away. There is nothing more unsettling than having what we felt as truth crumble beneath us. If it's no longer true that the dog owner is a selfish bastard, but a flawed human being just like me, what then do I do with the outrage? Who then am I to judge them so harshly? And how then do I stop them with a peaceful heart instead of a vengeful one? These are troublesome transitions.

The problems you face as a leader

I ran a survey of my social media followers and clients about their biggest people stuff challenges.[2]

Here are some of the answers to the question: *"What's your biggest struggle in dealing with other people?"*

- Saying one thing to my face but behaving differently
- Competing agendas
- Not getting 100% buy-in
- Managing passive-aggressive behaviour
- Making sure I don't offend by being a bit direct at times
- Poor communication, often caused by poor leadership, professional immaturity and people working in silos

---

2   Routh, Z. "People Stuff – help me write a great book – one that solves your problems". Survey 29 Sept, 2019.

- Being a policeman when two parties (staff members) have unsupportive and destructive behaviour
- Getting the difficult ones to leave and the good ones to stay (can I say that?!)
- Generational gaps. I am a young boomer and have a different work ethic to kids these days
- Considered 'too nice'
- People with no experience who keep trying to tell me how to do my job.

Like you, leaders struggle when others say or do things that they find troubling. Depending on our tolerance for conflict, this friction can be niggling through to traumatic. Worse, poor behaviour can escalate over time and become normalised.

Ultimately, this is what we really want:

- To do our job and do it well
- Contribute to something meaningful and feel proud of our work
- Share ideas, be heard and respected
- Learn, grow and have a sense of accomplishment
- Uplift others
- Be engaging and inspiring
- Guide positive change
- For our people to be happy at work
- For our people to play nice and share the toys.

As leaders, we are also mindful of not wanting to make things worse. We might be too emotional, or not emotional enough. We may be wound up too tight, ready to explode – or locked down, our inner world tucked away in an icebox. We might fear being too clinical, too tough, too direct. We worry that we might make the wrong decision. We know that we're not spending enough time on the big picture thinking, the future planning. We are in awe of leaders like

Elon Musk: leaders making the future real now. Leaders with real vision. What are *we* doing to make humanity better? Dealing with the day-to-day grind of problem solving and people stuff, we feel burdened and weighed down, our progress sluggish. Late at night, we worry that we might not be up to the task.

There is a gap between our aspirations and our current reality. This gap is filled with people stuff. Stuff that drains our energy, interferes with plans, and scuppers productivity. This gap can feel insurmountable.

I believe we can overcome differences. I believe that differences add to the beautiful tapestry of the work-life experience. I believe that when we look too closely at the individual threads, we see only how some are snagged, some are wound tight, and some are frayed. With perspective, we can zoom out to see the larger picture.

We need to shift our perspective so we can see what is driving the behaviour that we find irksome. There are often systems and context that generate the awkward people stuff. Once we can see the issues, we can fix them.

Leadership in crisis

Our immediate concerns with people stuff issues are set against a general cynicism towards leadership. This makes our job even harder, as we have few models of ethical and effective leadership in the public arena. We may also be tarred by the same brush: leaders are susceptible to pitfalls of power and corruption. As leaders, our people might eye us with the same suspicion.

We are experiencing a crisis of trust in leadership. We have fake news, stories generated for clickbait on the scantest of information, or even outright lies. We have alleged hacking of social media by foreign governments for political outcomes in other countries. We have uninformed opinions thrust upon us by supposed 'influencers'. The more of a social media following someone has, the more perceived trustworthiness they enjoy. Scary.

We have lost faith in our political leaders. Around the world, there is strong critique of government. For lack of a strong stance and action on climate change, for political corruption, for self-serving decision-making, for factionalism, for lack of vision.

We have lost faith in our business leaders. We look at the scandals related to WeWork and its astounding collapse, or the remarkable travesty of the Volkswagen saga, where deliberate deception of authorities for financial gain was systemic. And then in Australia we have the Royal Commission into Misconduct in the Banking, Superannuation and Financial Services Industry, where time and time again, across all the institutions, there was unethical behaviour: such as making up bank accounts, and charging for services that didn't exist. It's appalling.

We have lost faith in our religious leaders. The Royal Commission into Institutional Responses to Child Sexual Abuse has horrified us all. It is hard to have a sense of trust in leaders of institutions given the facts around these cases.

We have lost faith in public figures. The Weinstein incidents that launched the #MeToo movement exposed how power and its corrupting effects has had a negative impact on the previously voiceless masses.

We have lost faith in our leftist ideals. We are seeing a return to nationalist movements, to protect our own, to make our own country great again. We see this in America with Trump's populist sentiments. We see it in the United Kingdom with Brexit. Everywhere, many people are retreating from the global forum to look after their own particular, parochial, isolated concerns.

We have lost faith in media. Where is the independence in media? We see foreign interference in elections and propagation of false stories. We see Facebook refusing to take down fake news and misleading advertising and social media, because they feel that it's not their responsibility.

Trust in democracy is also eroding (*see Appendix A: Trust in public life*). According to research in *The Conversation*, "Fewer than 41% of

Australian citizens are satisfied with the way democracy works in Australia, down from 86% in 2007.[3]"

Our world view, how we see ourselves in the world and our purpose in it, has to change if we are going to survive our own innovations. We have to get beyond the election cycle planning of current politics. We need long-term strategic planning. We must rise above factionalism, nationalism, and protectionism, because we simply cannot escape the bonds that tie all of us together. All of us share ever-increasing points of connection. Our current political and government systems are not equipped and not agile enough to deal with the shocks that can come from these types of global crises. Our leaders are grossly ill-equipped to handle this kind of volatility.

The more connected we are, the more vulnerable we are. We are only as strong as our weakest member. Our resilience is tested not by the strong, but by the most frail amongst us. We cannot afford to think and operate in silos. Not in our businesses, not as nations.

The more connected we are, the more inclusive our thinking needs to be.

There's a lot to be worried about with our loss of faith in leadership generally, yet the people I work with are powerful leaders. They want to do the right thing. They're ethically driven. They are concerned about their community, they're concerned about their organisations, and they want to do good in the world. This gives me hope. This is the starting point.

We need the fundamentals of learning a new perspective, a new perspective on our values: who we are as leaders, how we see others and how we see the world. We need to see them first before we can adopt and adapt to this new context.

If we are to rebuild our faith in our political leaders, our institutions, our organisations, our value system, then we need to start from the inside-out. And that takes a rigorous self-examination to begin with. We need to examine how we see ourselves, how we see others and

---

[3] Australians' trust in politicians and democracy hits an all-time low: new research. (Ketchell, 2018)

how we see the world. Together, we can craft a new experience in this interconnected, amazing, modern day.

If only it was as easy as reframing how we look at dog shit. But it's a start.

Developmental frameworks for *People Stuff*

My perspective on leadership development and much of the work in this book has its root in integral leadership theory and models. The core concepts in these theories is that our individual and collective worldview can evolve in ever more inclusive and complex models of seeing and being in the world. Ken Wilber's insights[4] on cleaning up, growing up, waking up, and showing up is woven through much of this book.[5]

Cleaning up is about integrating shadows, or parts of us we have denied and suppressed that we end up projecting on others. When we integrate and deal with our shadow parts, it helps us to drop a lot of conflict we have in our personal and professional relationships.

Growing up is about shifting our perception of ourselves, others and the world to be more inclusive. It's when we realise that we each have a piece of the truth, and therefore truth is relative, and is dependent on our point of view.

Waking up is about discovering our true self; the part of us that is beyond our identities, our thoughts, our habits, our beliefs. It's about accessing the part of us that is the witness, the observer, the part of us that is beyond physical and temporal constraints. Anything we can see is not who we really are. It is sometimes described as pure awareness, consciousness or pure being.

Showing up is about doing work in service to the whole. As we exercise leadership in the smallest and biggest ways in each aspect of our

---

4 A great introduction to Ken Wilber's models can be found on various You Tube videos.
5 The great integral philosopher Ken Wilber is a core influence on my point of view and informs *People Stuff*. I have also immersed myself in and been inspired by the work of Don Beck and Christopher Cowan in *Spiral Dynamics* (1996, 2006), Bill Torbert's *Action Inquiry* (2004), and Susanne Cook-Greuter's *Leadership Maturity Framework*.

day-to-day life, we get to choose how we show up. It's a big calling. Leadership work, people stuff work, is confronting. We need to face demons, heal old wounds, practice forgiveness, and show courage.

Together we'll create the solution

I wrote *People Stuff* because I know leaders in organisations believe in their work and the benefit it provides their clients and the world. I believe they want to do the right thing and that they want to be a leader worth following. They want to be part of something great, to lead a team worth belonging to.

If you want to improve return on effort and decrease the time spent on people issues, this book is your pathway. With *People Stuff* in hand, you'll have:

- Less drain, more gain. Stop your interactions leaving you fed up; be freed up.

- Fewer complaints, better staff. Take your culture from crappy to happy.

- Save hours per week on staff issues. Turn your productivity from stuck to smooth.

Getting the people stuff right is no easy thing.

People stuff is messy. People stuff is hard. People stuff is prickly and rough. People stuff is slow and sluggish.

The secret, my friend, is perspective. We start there. How we see ourselves, others and the world directs our actions and determines our outcomes. Our perspective, our people insight, is our most important superpower. Everything cascades from there.

We want the ability to see as much as possible without losing sight of what is most important, and to make sense of it all. This is what we will be tackling.

How to use *People Stuff*

I've written this advanced handbook to be as practical as possible for leaders at all stages of their development. At the same time, I've also included depth for those who want more background and understanding of theory.

We start with maps of people stuff problems. When we have something like a map for the issues we have, it makes it easier to craft an approach that leads to better outcomes. The more maps we have, the more relaxed we can be as we can then read the patterns in the behaviour that we are experiencing. When we can read the territory, navigating it is a whole lot simpler.

The practice of perspective is our first map reading skill. It walks us through the different ways we can focus, kind of like adjusting the focus lens of a set of binoculars.

Next we take our map reading skills, zooming in and out of the issues from different angles, to help us develop new points of view. There are three points of view on people stuff we aim to develop in this book:

- YOU: Perspective on the self
- THEM: Perspective on others
- US: Perspective on the bigger things

Each section tackles the subject with a case study or story from the 'Boardroom'. The Boardroom describes experiences from the trenches, from real leaders dealing with real issues. In most cases I have changed names and details, created a composite, and fictionalised the story to protect privacy, as the issues are often sensitive.

The Boardroom section is followed by the 'Big Picture' explanation. Here we take a deeper dive into the complexity of the dynamics at play. This is for the reader who wants to geek out on dynamics and models to make sense of the people stuff. 'Brass Tacks' is where we boil it all down to practical things you can implement. For those who just want to cut to the chase, you can flip to the end of each chapter and get what you need there.

I've included a Q&A section to demonstrate how to apply your map reading skills to the actual territory of people stuff, with real issues from real leaders.

If you want to explore further, there is the resource section where you can dig into the topics that niggle or excite you.

Let us begin.

PART TWO

The practice of perspective

Checking in

When tackling our practice of perspective, the first step is to check in with where you are as a leader. We are at all at various stages of our leadership maturity and the associated insight 'superpower'. Let's see where you sit.

Are you feeling blind?

- You take everyone at their word and are disappointed when they don't follow through.

- You feel fed up and fried. People don't do what they're told, can't work it out for themselves, and don't want to take any responsibility.

- Every time you look around, people are drinking coffee, chatting and not getting on with what they're supposed to be doing – work! You feel the culture is lazy.

Blindness is what keeps us feeling stuck. Being blind to the people stuff means we are ill-equipped to deal with or prevent the people stuff issues that affect productivity. We keep thinking it's a personality problem.

When we're blind to the people stuff, we don't see the dynamics at play, how they emerged, or what drives the systems that creates the frictions. We devalue our people, instead of digging a little deeper into causes of their disappointing behaviour. All we know is that work sucks and people are unhappy, including us.

Blinkered?

- Productivity is slow. You can't see what is getting in the way, and you can't seem to optimise systems and processes to release blocks.

- You are frustrated. You sense the solution is just outside your awareness, but you don't know what it is.

- You feel the culture is dull.

Our bias creates blinkers. Our thinking style, behaviour preferences, background, language, values all create filters that build up to create these blinkers. If we can't see the obstacles to unity, nor the value of diversity, we are at risk of condemning our teams and workplaces to grey blandness. Culture can only become vibrant when we unite common focus and celebrate our differences.

... or feeling bionic?

- Your insight smooths the path. You see friction before it arises and can tweak systems to release productivity problems before they become blocks.

- Interactions are freed up. People enjoy your company, and you theirs. You can have robust disagreements and know the relationships are only strengthened. You are free to be yourself and encourage others the same way.

- You know the culture is vibrant. When people are seen, heard, and valued, they cannot help but feel happy. The work we do on how we see ourselves, them, and the bigger picture, helps us appreciate others, no matter how different to us.

Heightened awareness makes us seem bionic. When we have this insight, it's as if we have enhanced abilities that give us laser sharp observational skills and fast savvy solutions to tricky problems. It's this awareness we need to work towards.

So, how did you go? Blind, blinkered or both? No matter where you sit, we have work to do to create your super-charged bionic People Stuff insight. Let's start with the story of Jimmy.

BOARDROOM CASE STUDY
Island time

Jimmy was avoiding me. He did not appear at breakfast and skipped the morning masterclass on delegation. We were five days into an eight-day leadership intensive and his participation was becoming ever more erratic.

At last I found him, drinking coffee in a corner.

"Jimmy! How are you?" He blinked at me with weary eyes. It looked like he'd had a sleepless night.

"You missed the masterclass this morning. What happened?" He looked at this coffee for what seemed like a very long moment.

"I'm finding the course hard. I'm not sure it's right for me."

"Can you tell me more?" Another long pause.

"We do things differently in the Torres Strait."

"How do you mean?"

"When we ask someone to share their story, it's an important thing. We don't have written traditions. We're an oral culture. It's how we share our knowledge and wisdom. To interrupt someone when they tell their story is the height of rudeness."

I sat stunned. He was talking about the previous night's session. The group had been tasked with sharing their life journey, with key challenges and triumphs, and the insights they gained through it. They'd been given ten minutes each to do so. No one stuck to time. Each participant's story grew longer and longer. It was nearing midnight and I was fretting about the impact on the following day, and especially on my personal energy. As the third last participant, also from the Torres Strait, was reaching close to 45 minutes in his story, I spoke up and asked him if he might conclude so we could move on to the two remaining participants. He was startled, and then quickly finished his tale. I was relieved. We concluded the exercise not long after that and headed to bed.

I sat with Jimmy's words, dumbfounded. I had no such reference point for storytelling and respect. I had been taught, 'wait your turn, don't hog the limelight, and keep to time'. For Jimmy, storytelling was an essential survival tool. It was therefore not only rude but stupid to interrupt. For me, interrupting to keep to time was being respectful to the others in the group.

I saw the participant's behaviour as disrespectful; he saw mine as disrespectful. It all stemmed from how we perceived time and storytelling. It was a clash of worldviews: different values, different perspectives.

It never occurred to me that what I held as 'common courtesy' was a made-up idea, a construct. I thought everybody knew that being on time was the done thing: make a plan, set a specific time appointment, show up on time or early. As far as I knew, not sticking to time, being late, was the height of rudeness.

I listened to Jimmy a while longer as he told me more and more what it was like to navigate white western culture from a different vantage point. He told me that Islanders relate differently to time. It's known as 'Island Time'. When the time feels right, people gather to get things done, share stories, have meetings. The western concept of being on time, sticking to time, and arriving for an appointment at a particular time was not relevant nor practised. Life and work were neither linear nor boxed.

Wow. It was such a gift to be shown how our views, our perspective, can blind us to what others are experiencing, and how this can cause huge rifts and conflict.

From then I became curious about how to explore perspective – ours and that of others – so that we can better understand one another and build better solutions that suit more of us.

BIG PICTURE

Working towards the practice of perspective

Perspective is seeing, experiencing, and making meaning.

It's how we look at something, where we look from, and the story we tell about it.

It's a point of view.

It's an experience and an interpretation of it.

It's a dance between objectivity and relativity.

We can't look at anything without using filters. We all have filters. Perspective is shaped by our past experiences, values and beliefs. It's the collective lens, made of layers upon layers of stories, through which we choose to see the world. Sometimes we have names for these collective filters that are common ways of seeing the world, words like liberalism, communism, socialism, conservatism, and progressiveness.

These filters allow us to make judgments and decisions. These filters are designed to preserve our own self-interest and survival. Sometimes this is useful, sometimes it is not. Useful filters are when they assess an imminent threat, like 'that person advancing towards me is a menace'. We take action accordingly. Less useful filters make us judgmental, as in the case with Jimmy, and we open the window to bias and misunderstanding.

The practice of perspective

When Jimmy dropped the bombshell of awareness on me, I started wondering how can we see more of our blind spots? How can we discover the lenses through which we are seeing ourselves, others, and the world?

Things we assume are true don't get challenged, because we 'know' them to be true. Things like the sun rises every morning, the sky is blue, fire is hot. We have substantial and quantifiable evidence for these facts. When it comes to people stuff, the same thing occurs. We gather evidence, consciously or not, to support what we assume are truths. This is unconscious bias at work. There are lots of reasons why this is helpful. Being able to make sense of a huge amount of data through pattern recognition is how our species has survived and accelerated its evolutionary success: we developed neural shortcuts to help us quickly assess who or what is a threat and who is not. Daniel Kahneman's Nobel Prize-winning work in *Thinking Fast and Slow* (2011) revealed the benefits and challenges of our grey matter's processing power. It's helpful to have shortcuts and make assumptions about many things. Except when we get it wrong. Like I did with Jimmy.

So then, how do we rein in our big beautiful brains? How do we become more aware of the automatic assumptions that derail us and create false conclusions? We need to become aware of our thinking processes and challenge them.[6]

This is no easy thing. Like fish swimming in water, at first we do not know there are filters, or 'water'. Until we become aware that we are experiencing the world through multiple lenses, we assume the world we see is unfiltered, plain as day. The practice of perspective is about developing our ability to see more of the picture, filters and all, so we can make smarter, wiser decisions.

A note before we proceed. It's a long way off the people stuff track, but stick with me: *perspective is a powerful meta skill that will shape and shake the fundamentals of your leadership practice.* Ultimately, it will make the immediate concerns of people stuff easier, and more effective.

But first, let's brave the wilderness and wander through the vast unknown. Your map reading and compass skills will help you make it through the people stuff jungle. It's like preparing for a day hike with your team and wondering why we need to study the geological forces of the Himalayas, weather patterns of the last two centuries, and history of the Nepalese people before you go. The short answer: you'll pack a better pack, you'll have a nicer trip, and you'll survive the expedition.

---

6   For an excellent text that showcases the glitches in our thinking, David Robson's *The Intelligence Trap – Why Smart People Do Dumb Things*, is a worthy read.

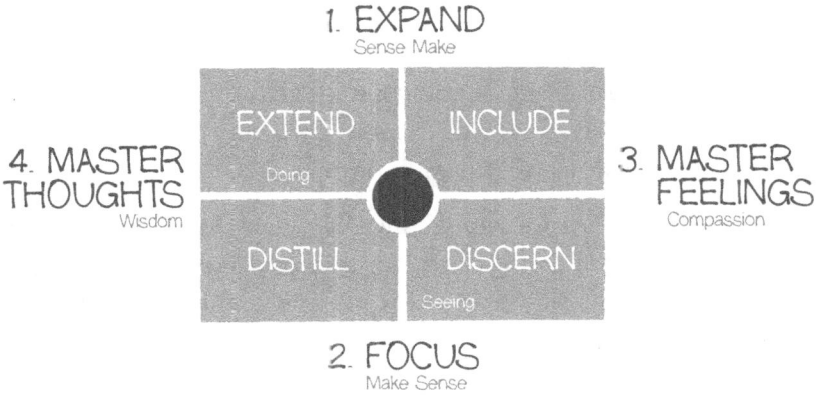

Figure 1: Model of the practice of perspective

Your leadership navigation tool: The practice of perspective map

For as long as we've gazed up at the stars, we've had ways of making sense of where we are, and where we might go next. As a species, we first used the natural world to guide our explorations: stars, tides, rivers, seasons. Then we developed instruments to make our journeys more accurate and reliable. Sailors used an astrolabe to gauge the angle of the sun and a known star from the horizon. This way they could calculate their latitude while sailing. We've had the compass that aligns to magnetic north and helps us see which way we are facing. Used in conjunction with maps, these tools help us travel through vast wildernesses and across oceans.

What we are contending with now as leaders is much like what the first explorers faced: a horizon with unknown destinations, and unknown dangers. We also have great resources at hand to help us make wise and compassionate decisions.

The practice of perspective map is our navigation tool to make better choices in the moment, and for the long haul.

Let's walk through the map in Figure 1.

The vertical axis is the 'seeing' line. We want to be able to see far and wide, as well as zoom in to the here and now. The 'expand' end of the axis is like using a giant telescope to see into the depths of the universe. The 'focus' end helps us look at what is right here in front of us, like using a magnifying glass or microscope.

The horizontal axis is the 'doing' line. As leaders we need not only to be able to see what is going on, but to take effective and meaningful action. Imagine an old-fashioned scale. One end balances the best of our mind – wisdom – and the other end balances the best of our heart – compassion. We need both, otherwise we make unbalanced choices. Cindy Wigglesworth calls this 'spiritual intelligence'. She defines it this way in her amazing book, *SQ21 – The Twenty-One Skills of Spiritual Intelligence* (2012): *"[Spiritual intelligence] is the ability to behave with wisdom and compassion, while maintaining inner and outer peace, regardless of the situation."* For me, this is the ideal we should be aiming for in all of our leadership practice.

Each axis point has a set of skills to develop. We explore these in detail in the next section.

The seeing and doing axis, along with their core skills, create four core leadership principles: include, extend, discern, decide. We will discuss each in turn as we go through the map.

We will begin from the top.

1. Let's start with expand: sense-making

Sense-making is trying to see what is really going on.

At the top of the model, we have 'expand'. We want to see as much and as far as possible. This is about expanding our perspective. Think big. Think horizons. Think deep space and beyond! Our intention is to see as much as possible, from as many angles as possible, over the longest time horizon, past and future. This gives us better insight into challenges and helps spot opportunities.

There are three dimensions we explore in the 'expand' part of our map: time, complexity, and meaning.

1. Time

With the time dimension, we want to see what patterns have led to where we are today. Then we want to see how far our actions might reach into the future. How far back (or forward) can we go? This is a great mental exercise to help us expand our sense-making when it comes to time. This section is inspired by Tim Urbain's posts on his website *Wait But Why* (www.waitbutwhy.com). He does a marvellous job at putting things in perspective. I've used his approach to help explore the idea that all things are relative.

Consider your life in a 24-hour chunk, made up of one-hour chunks, and the concept of 'Now' in the middle.

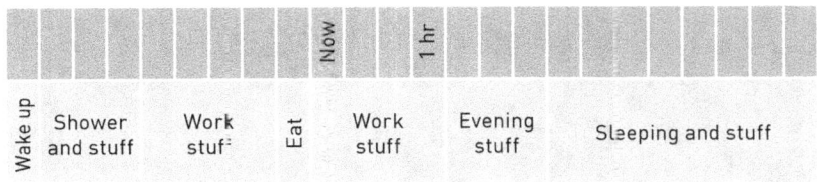

'Now' is when a significant event happens in your working day, like a disagreement or a bad meeting. In this instance it's an upset staff member, Karen. Karen walks into your office and has a bitch about Frank. It was tough listening to her rant. She went on and on about how he does not respect her, tramples on her feelings, and interferes with her work area.

It was but a single one-hour chunk in your day, but it had a big impact.

Each hour has 3,600 seconds. Each day has 86,400 seconds. Since every decision is made in the moment, every feeling is experienced now, that's a lot of opportunity to choose something and do something.

In the Now, you listened to Karen for 3,600 seconds, and then felt worried about the fallout and what to do about it for the following three days, or 259,200 seconds.

This is how we trace impact of our thoughts and actions: little ones, made in the moment, followed by another little one, made in another little moment.

Let's put your 'Now' into an even bigger perspective:

Consider your day relative to all of your days, if you lived to 80. You'd have 29,220 days all up. If you turn 50 this year, as I am, that means on your 50th birthday, you'd have had 18,261 days used up already (assuming I calculated the leap years correctly), leaving you 10,959 days (or 946,857,600 seconds) to go. There are 365 days fitting into one box. It looks something like this:

At 50, you potentially have less days ahead of you than you have behind. It tends to sharpen your focus a little! You might pay a little more attention to what matters most, and less on stuff that doesn't (in theory anyway).

That's one little life. But we are all dangling on the end of an enormous chain of lives that came before us.

How many generations of your family tree do you know? How many names can you remember? I know up to my grandparents' names: Naomi, Edgar, Edith, and Maurice. That's it. Three generations. My grandfather was born in 1920. As I write this book, my current personal memory expands 100 years. Let's look at this within the calendar since we started counting years after Christ's birth.

A lot of history happened over the last 20 centuries: Genghis Khan, Queen Elizabeth I, a few plagues, the rise and fall of several Empires, electricity, plumbing, the bicycle, space travel, and twerking.

But there's a whole bunch of other human stories that came before these amazing events. Let's look now at Aboriginal cultural history in Australia. There are different timelines as to when the first people arrived in Australia, so let's go with 65,000 years cited in a 2017 archaeological study[7].

In the two graphs below, each of the boxes represents 2,000 years.

---

7   Clarkson, C and Jacobs, Z. 20 July 2017. Human occupations of northern Australia by 65,000 years ago, *Nature*.

The entire graph of the last 2,000 years, from Caesar to Trump, fits mostly in the last box. We make much of European and North American history, but it pales in duration compared with our first peoples. As the longest living cultures in human history, they have carried collective insight and wisdom over multiple 2,000-year periods.

Let's look now at Aboriginal history compared with the history of humanity. Modern humans are said to have emerged some 200,000 years ago.

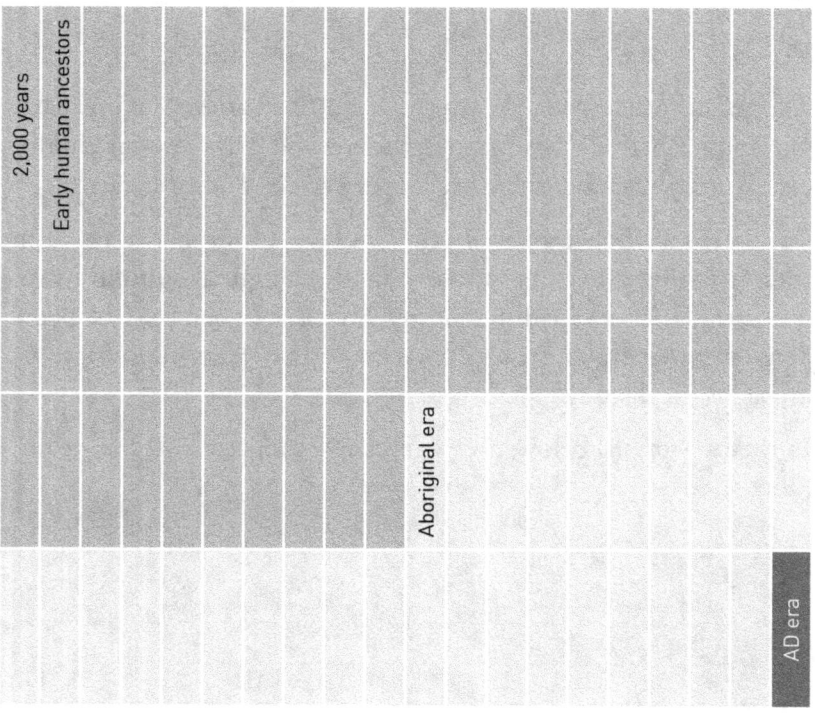

Makes you wonder about life for ancient ancestors, Gork and Gack, 200,000 years ago. Did they have Monday-itis? Arguments over who let the fire go out again? Bad hair days? Did they entertain themselves with a round of charades and shadow puppets on cave walls? Did they spend nights staring up at the stars, wondering …

That's a lot of humans, over a very long time. If Gack hadn't met Gork and given him a subtle eyebrow raise in the dim firelight flicker, there might not have been little Zoë millennia later. There's a lot of happy accidents that have led to where we are today. A lot of small choices in tiny moments.

Considering the scale and depth of this rolling stone of humanity does two things for perspective:

1. Reminds us simultaneously that our lives are whispers of nothing in time, and that they matter. To those we care about, and to those we'll never know.
2. What seems insignificant can be momentous.

As leaders, we need to weave this polarity and paradox into our perspective: the here and now with where and next.

Apart from being an interesting intellectual exercise, we want to answer the question, 'so what?' How does exploring time in perspective help us with our troubles now with Karen and Frank?

Inspiring leaders are masters of sense-making.

When we show the story of where we fit and how we fit, as leaders we can elevate spirit and call forward the best in others. Why is honing the practice of perspective so important?

Perspective humbles.

When we see ourselves relative to the greater experience of the universe, we know that our individual micro experience is nothing in the big picture. We are a miracle of accidents and coincidences that is beyond the scope of our rational understanding.

Perspective sharpens focus.

If we only have but a brief life in the timeline horizon of the universe, we need to make the most of it! We waste so much time forgetting life is miraculous.

Awe helps sharpen our sense of service.

When we experience our place in the world from a place of humility, of deep admiration that evokes a sense of awe, we feel pulled to serve a higher purpose, one that looks after the people, planet, and place. Connection trumps isolation.

Before we move into the focus end of the seeing axis, we need to understand the big picture from different angles. This is when we start to look at patterns through time.

We look at trends from the past, and into the future. We use environmental scanning – called STEEPOE – to help us sense-make across time, past, present, and future.

A framework for sense-making: STEEPOE

Futurists have wonderful frameworks to help us expand perspective. One of them is called environmental scanning, or STEEPOE.

- Social trends: What are the patterns we are seeing in demographics, structures of the population, patterns of work, gender roles, age roles and needs, consumers, and cultural practices?

- Technological trends: What are the emerging and past experiences and application of technology? What is happening with cost, accessibility, integration, adoption, production of tech?

- Economic trends: What is/has been happening with respect to economic prosperity and growth, inflation, interest rates, international trade agreements and laws, employment rates, and fundamentals of national and international economic drivers?

- Environmental trends: What's happening in global weather patterns? How is climate change affecting local and global animal and people's behaviour? What is happening with seasonal shifts? How is human development affecting and interacting with the natural world?

- Political trends: What is happening globally on different political stages? What kind of legislation is being passed and repealed locally, nationally, and globally? How are governments being nominated, challenged, or replaced? What is happening with government services and taxation?
- Organisational trends: How are organisations treating their people? What role do businesses see themselves playing in society, economy and the world? What systems are being used for recruitment, employment, culture, remuneration? Are organisations getting bigger, smaller, local or remote? How are the laws changing that affect employment arrangements? How are unions and trade agreements evolving?
- Ethical trends: What are the major concerns of advocacy groups? What's changing in advocacy? What are the major concerns that are being voiced across communities? How are leaders responding to or articulating their ethical standpoints?

Remember we are still in 'expand' at this point. We are sense-making, seeing patterns across time. We have not yet moved to making sense when we start to ask the question, 'now what?' As part of expand, we move from looking at time and patterns across time, to look at complexity.

2. Complexity

It wasn't a linear path from Gack and Gork to Zoë. It's not a chain reaction, like dominos falling.

The evolution of human civilisation is a dynamic interaction of various systems: social, technological, ecological, economic, political, organisational, and ethical. The STEEPOE exercise helped us to see some of those patterns. We need to dive a little deeper into the complexity of the systems that create the patterns.

It's like looking at the human body. Looking at exercise, diet, shape, size, and ability, we can see patterns of behaviours and outcomes. STEEPOE allows this kind of insight: what can we observe in the conditions in front of us? If we are to understand a little more of what we are seeing, we need to take a look at the systems creating these observable outcomes. In the human body, this might be the respiratory system, the digestive system, the circulatory system, and how they are interacting. In people stuff, we look at the politics, culture, administration, goal setting, and other functions of the organisation.

People stuff problems are often oversimplified without looking at the systems: we give them a task, they should do it. If they don't, they're either incompetent or insubordinate!

When Karen whinged about Frank, we might be tempted to call it a personality problem.

People stuff is rarely about personality; it's more often about process.

If we are to solve people stuff problems, we need to look at the systems that are creating those friction points.

Systems thinking is a way of making visible the complex dynamics of a situation. Organisations are systems: a complex set of rules and relationships that produce results, some wanted, some unwanted. When we map these dynamics, we see better where weaknesses and blockages are. We can also see leverage points and thresholds.

To map an organisational system, we start with a result, like 'happy staff'. Now we mindmap cause/effect relationships affecting this outcome. We also map the effect of happy staff on other aspects of the organisational system. The end result looks like a bowl of spaghetti, with some components being a bit more tangled. These are 'hot spots'.

There are two types of hot spots: causal and outcome. Causal hot spots are ones that have more arrows coming out of them than in. This means that this result has an impact on many other parts of the organisation. This is a potential leverage point. An outcome hot spot is one where there are many arrows going into that spot. This means there are a lot of contributing factors affecting that particular result. If we change an element of a causal hot spot, we can create ripple effects through the system.

Before doing a systems map, we might guess at what the problems were between Karen and Frank. She complained that he was not taking her opinion seriously, he spoke over the top of her, and that he was interfering in her operational area. On the surface of it, it looks like it is a temperament problem and Frank needs to be told to pull his head in.

I made a simple systems map to illustrate this flow. Designed for a mythical organisation called Happy Pants Company, where Karen and Frank work, you can see where the hot spots are.

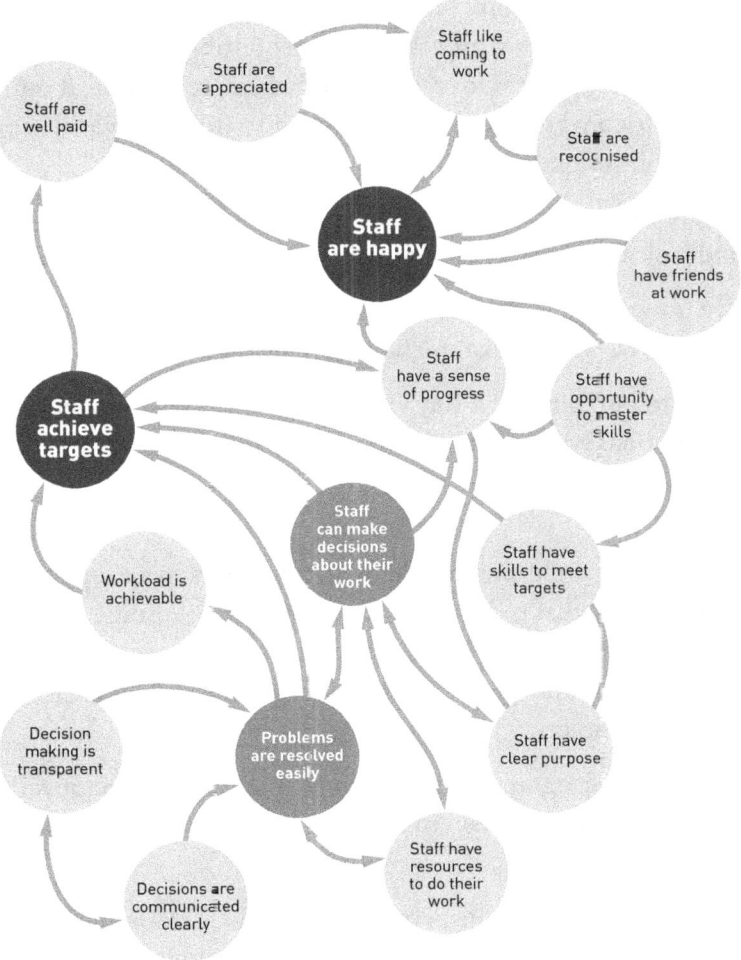

Figure 2: The dynamics in the system of the Happy Pants Company

29

The black ringed hot spots are OUTCOME hot spots. These are the key results we're after: happy staff and staff achieving their targets. Since Karen is not happy, we can look into the systems map and see what might be causing this outcome.

There are two hot spots in grey that have more arrows coming out of them. These are CAUSAL hot spots. In this map, it's 'staff can make decisions about their work' and 'problems are resolved easily.'

The work of the leader is to examine the boundaries around decision-making and problem solving for each team member. Where can they have more autonomy? Do they need to develop more guidelines about decision-making processes and responsibilities? Do they need to have a better process for resolving glitches? Do they need training in difficult conversations? Do they need to do some work around expectations of one another?

If we are looking for people stuff opportunities and challenges, we would look to tweak these hubs to cause positive effects in our systems.

We've gone from surface challenges between Frank and Karen, to looking at the systems that might be driving the wedge between them.

It's time to pull out our X-Ray vision and look at what underpins the organisational systems themselves: values and meaning.

3. Meaning

When we look at chronic problems and successes in an organisation, we want to see what is driving historic and future results. All choices are based on values and beliefs. To use our bionic seeing skills, we look with our X-Ray vision at the underpinning values creating the systems and choices.

When we look again at the systems map for the Happy Pants Company, we need to keep in mind that values come in two forms: aspirational and actual.

If we were to interview the people at Happy Pants Company and ask them what is important to the company as a whole, they might say something like:

- Being a great place to work
- Everyone belonging
- People enjoying working with each other
- Kicking goals.

These are clear in the systems map. If we then ask them what gets in the way of these outcomes, we might hear things like:

"We are very competitive with one another. We have bonuses tied to performance, so that means we need to fight a little to get the resources we need. We've even had people steal clients across departments to meet their targets. Friendly rivalry turned to bitter competition."

Aha. This puts the challenges between Frank and Karen in a new light. The reward and remuneration system was having an impact on their behaviour and interactions. Competition over collaboration was the outcome.

So, the *actual* values being articulated in the system are:

- Profit before people
- Win regardless of the cost
- Targets trump harmony.

Not many leaders would choose these values deliberately. And yet they are there, expressed in the system. This is an opportunity for leaders to ask: "what do we really value? Do our systems support what we say we believe in? What needs to be changed? What needs to stay the same? What needs to be enhanced?"

Now that we have looked at time, complexity, and meaning, we are getting ready to zoom in to the 'focus' part of our perspective practice map. Before we do that, let's review the 'expand' component:

Tools for sense-making

There are three guiding principles for expanding our perspective:

1. *Think of trends.* Expand the review of trends affecting the current situation. Expand the projection of effects into future generations.

2. *Think in systems.* Challenges are often complex. The best way to understand them is to map dynamics, pressures, and thresholds.

3. *Think about meaning.* Ask: what are the values being supported or expressed in this challenge and decision?

All of this sense-making takes effort and time. That's why so many leaders don't do it. It's hard to prioritise work that feels vast and nebulous. Sense-making is fumbling in the fog for patterns, signals of what is happening and where we might go. It's not as rewarding as ticking off something on the task list. It's a formless blob, difficult to grasp, and leaves us steeped in ambiguity and tangled in complexity.

And yet do the work of sense-making we must. If we don't, we walk blind. We blunder into cultural faux pas. We miss opportunities. We get disrupted and languish behind our competitors. When we do the work of sense-making, we zoom out far and wide and deep. We look for patterns in the points. Then we start to make connections and see potential pathways.

2. Next, it's time to Focus: We need to make sense

On the other side of expanding perspective is making sense. When we dial our lens on Figure 1 on page 19 from 'expand' down to 'focus', we determine what to make of all these amazing points of view, and what we should do next. This requires us to focus.

Focus is freeing. Focus helps us zoom in on what matters most and make a solid decision. Here again we can turn to the Futurists[8]. They have a toolbox of filters that help us distil the vast array of information and data into something practical that can help us anticipate and plan for the future. It's a huge competitive advantage.

Useful filters include scenario planning, problem trees, and listing assumptions. This will help us map complexity and reveal opportunities.

---

8 There are many wonderful Futurist resources and communities. A good place to start is the World Future Society: www.worldfuture.org. There is also list of good books in the Resources section. And many science fiction writers are in fact Futurists! Arthur C Clarke is a great example. So if you want to know a little about the future, read some science fiction!

Filter 1: Scenario planning

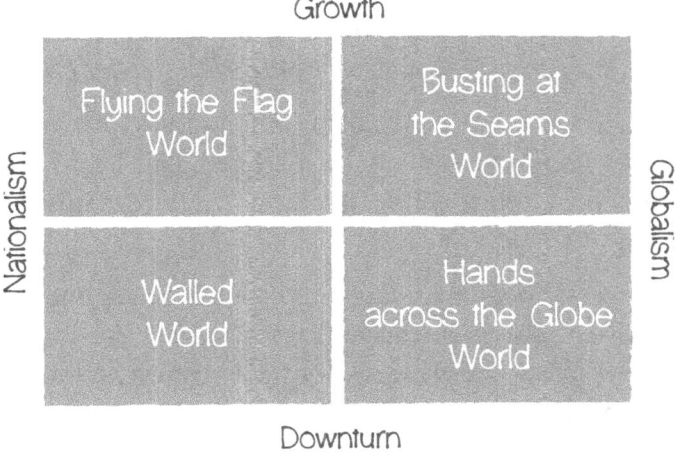

Figure 3: Sample scenario planning

Let's start with scenario planning. We have a sample scenario plan in Figure 3. Let's walk through how we build this and what do with it.

To craft a scenario plan, take a look at the STEEPOE trends. Which are the ones that are the most volatile? These are the ones with the greatest uncertainty, and the greatest likelihood of wreaking havoc in our business or organisation. Pick two to start and then map them on a vertical and horizontal axis, with extremes of each trend at either pole.

In Figure 3 we chose the political trends of globalism for one end of a pole and nationalism for the other. These are two major competing trends in the zeitgeist. For the other axis we chose global economic downturn and global economic growth. We now have four possible scenarios.

- Scenario 1 – Downturn and nationalism. This leads to defensiveness, a rise in protectionism, hostility towards migrants and refugees, cautious spending, and conservative business building. We might call this *Walled World*.

- Scenario 2 – Growth and nationalism. This leads to civic pride, aggressive economic expansion and trade negotiations, and an increase in government services. We might call this *Flying the Flag World*.

- Scenario 3 – Downturn and globalism. This leads to possible increased cooperation between countries, and an increase in diplomatic activity to reassure and protect existing trade deals or broker new ones. We could call this *Hands Across the Globe World*.
- Scenario 4 – Growth and globalism. This leads to an increase in global workforce mobilisation, increased global emissions, and strain on transport and infrastructure services. This could be *Busting at the Seams World*.

We can then evaluate the scenarios for the ones we like and ones that are likely. We've seen elements of these in our current context. The COVID-19 epidemic is driving significant downturn across the globe. Trends of Nationalism and Globalism will determine whether we get Walled World or Hands Across the Globe. Which world do you like? Which do you think is likely? What might you do as a leader?

The best futurists do more than one set of scenarios. After evaluating the scenarios above, we now generate actions to contend with unwanted outcomes of the trends, or promote the likelihood of the scenarios we'd prefer. The ethos is 'forewarned is forearmed.' We need to rinse and repeat the process with multiple trends. Scenario planning is good for generating options in broad contexts, like the one we've created above. It also serves our more immediate context. We can pick trends affecting our local area or industry sector to create scenarios closer to home.

Scenarios are good for pre-empting problems and spotting opportunities. Problem trees helps us diagnose more immediate issues and make plans to deal with them.

Filter 2: Problem trees

Problem trees help us map what drives visible problems. Often leaders will try and solve presenting problems from what looks like obvious surface solutions. It's like putting a Band-Aid on an internal haemorrhage. To create your problem tree, start with a visible problem. Here's a people stuff example: The executive team are at each other's throats.

Let's look at Frank and Karen again.

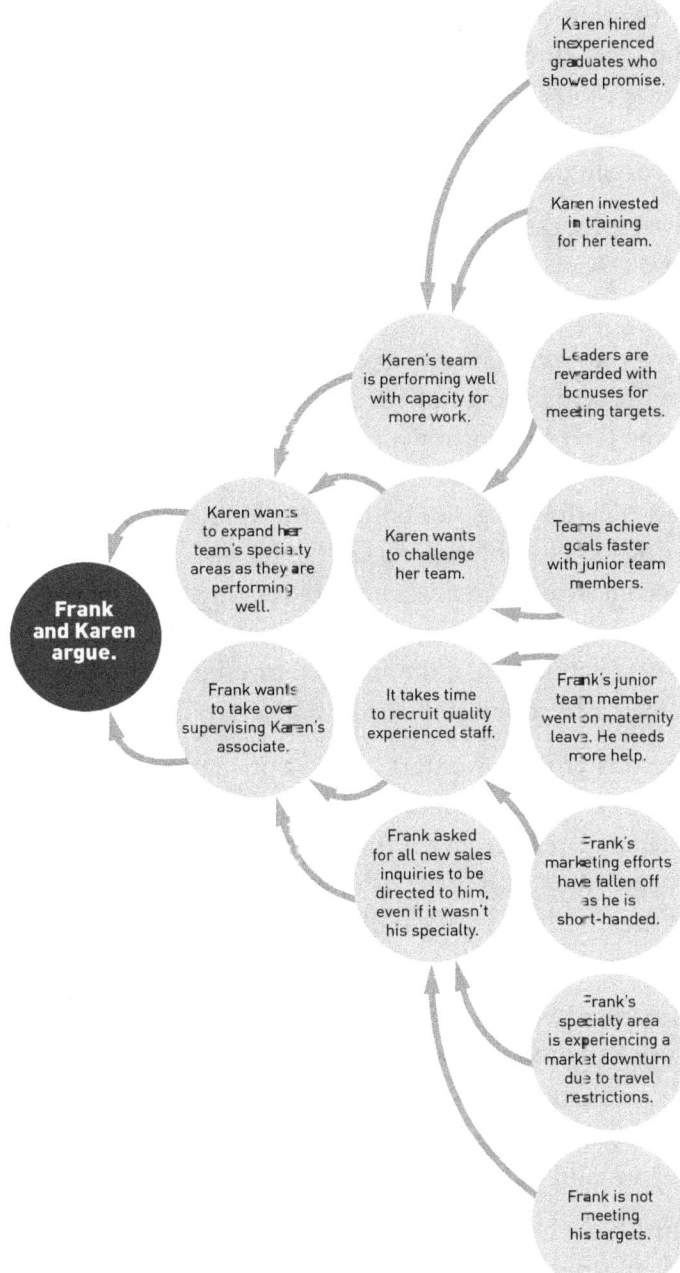

Figure 4: Problem tree for Frank and Karen

We list the presenting problem at the top of a whiteboard or piece of paper – "Frank and Karen argue". Next we ask: what are two factors that are creating this tension? We list them under the first problem, with directional lines from the two factors back up to the presenting problem, like roots feeding into a stem. In this case, we see that Frank wants to take a resource from Karen's team just as she seeks to expand it.

Then we repeat the process with each of these two factors: why does Frank want Karen's associate? Why does Karen want to expand her team's specialty areas?

Following the roots down, we discover that a downturn in the market, along with being short-staffed, has led Frank to miss meeting his targets and then coming under financial pressure. Karen is motivated to expand her team because she has recruited and trained well and the team is performing. For both Frank and Karen, rewards are tied to meeting targets. Through no fault of his own, Frank finds himself losing income while Karen sees hers accelerating. Even though they are colleagues in the same company, self-interest is driving competition instead of collaboration. If they worked together, they could solve the resourcing problem across the board and all would meet their targets.

In doing this process, we start to see contributing factors that were not obvious above the surface. In this case, one of the weeds choking team harmony stems from the financial incentives of meeting targets. When people are confronted with survival threats, they do not always express their best selves. We will see more of this in the chapter on the Four Devils of people stuff.

As leaders then, we must deal first with the effect of tension between Frank and Karen. We can uncover the competing interests and work towards a collaborative solution. Then we can solve the issue and prevent it occurring again by re-designing the remuneration strategy. This way we pull the weed out by the roots.

Our third filter helps turn on the bionic X-Ray vision once again. We look at assumptions in our thinking. Instead of looking at the problem itself, we look at how we are looking at the problem.

Filter 3: List and challenge assumptions

When we do scenario planning and problem trees, assumptions guide our choices. We must be rigorous in our approach to ensure we don't get derailed by an assumption that has no basis. So, we make assumptions (guesses) about which trends are the most important and volatile. We then make assumptions about which scenario is most likely to occur. When using problem trees, we make assumptions about the contributing causes. It's important that we challenge these assumptions to make sure we have created the best possible options for action.

Here's how to tackle assumptions in the Frank and Karen situation, after we have completed the problem tree. Starting from the top, we make assumptions about Frank and Karen's relationship. Because Karen spent an hour in the office complaining about Frank, we might list the following assumptions:

- Things are getting bad
- Karen doesn't know how to resolve it with Frank
- Frank is difficult to approach

All of these may be true, but it's important we list them to show where we are filling in assumptions, and where we have facts. Looking at the next layer down the problem tree, we have listed what Frank and Karen have said outright: Frank wants to take one of Karen's resources, and Karen wants to expand her specialty areas. These are facts, not assumptions. The story we might tell about this is:

Karen and Frank are both ambitious. They are also both acting in silos. In the next level down (where Frank wants to field all inquiries first, even outside of his speciality area), we might make the assumption: Why should Frank get access to all new business? This is not equitable or fair. Frank is desperate. Frank is selfish. Frank is not a team player.

With Karen, we might make the assumption that Karen is looking out for her team and she is leading them well.

It's only at this last layer we start to see two possible stories emerging for Frank: He is not meeting his targets, his speciality area is experiencing a downturn, his marketing efforts are failing, and he is short-handed. We could interpret this as Frank is not competent and people don't like to be on his team. That's one story. The alternative is that Frank is unlucky as he has been sabotaged by both a market downturn and staff shortage.

On Karen's side, there are also two possible stories that might emerge:

Karen has invested in training for promising graduates. As a result, we see her team achieve goals as well as financial rewards for leaders hitting targets. One story about these facts is that Karen is a smart and savvy leader who sees the long-term benefit of growing a competent team. Another story is that Karen is a smart, self-oriented leader who will set herself up for success by leveraging the resources available to her.

There are many possible stories here. Frank is incompetent and desperate; Karen is competent and capable. Frank is a victim of circumstance and systems; Karen is an ambitious ladder climber.

Our relationship with both of them and our perception of their personality may affect how we handle the situation, and therefore the outcomes for not only Frank and Karen, but for the organisation. By listing our assumptions and taking an X-Ray, we can press pause on judgment and stay focused on what is really going on. When we get to the chapter on the Four Devils, we will learn more about the patterns of behaviour we may be witnessing and responding to.

Summary of filters for Focus

On the Focus end of the Seeing axis in Figure 1, we exercise our perspective to zoom into what are the most important and salient issues to resolve. There are three useful filters to help us distill the most important aspects of a challenge:

Filter 1. Scenario planning. When we map potential futures, it gives us possibilities to choose from. It helps us to anticipate problems and see opportunities.

Filter 2. Problem tree. When we trace the problem back to its roots, we see below the surface of the immediate issue. This helps us choose actions that can cause long-term improvements and avoid Band-Aid solutions.

Filter 3. List assumptions. When we expose the stories we tell about a situation, we bring some of our biases to light. This helps us avoid quick judgments and stay focused on identifying the best path forward.

Now that we have expanded our perspective to the biggest picture possible through time, complexity, and meaning, then zoomed into focus through the use of different filters like scenario planning, problem trees and listing assumptions, we can move to the next component of the practice of perspective: the doing part.

In the next two quadrants of the practice of perspective (see to the left and right of Figure 1 on page 24), we are in the domain of doing: taking action that is both sensible and sensitive. This is the rubber hitting the road. We've got to start making decisions and doing stuff. Because we are values-driven and caring folk, we want to do this the best way we can.

The lens of doing swings between acting with wisdom and acting with compassion. It's how we balance being sensible and being sensitive.

3. Mastering thoughts, or the art of being sensible and wise

In the third quadrant of the practice of perspective (to the left in Figure 1), we ask ourselves: how do we make decisions that are wise? This has been a question for leaders everywhere since time immemorial. It is best paraphrased as: "how do I make a decision that won't suck and stuff things up?"

We can only know in retrospect whether a decision was wise or not. However, we can rinse our decisions through useful filters. Sense-making and making sense helps us see more of the picture in which we find ourselves. After we have expanded our view and then focused our lens, we can use these guiding principles to master our thoughts and filter our decision-making process. On the left-hand side of the quadrant model, we will apply wisdom principles to sense making. This helps us EXTEND our scope of concern.

We will also apply wisdom principles to the making sense pole, and this will help us DECIDE on what to do next.

Wisdom principles

To be wise is to make the best possible choice given what we know and can see at this current time. What makes it the best choice is the biggest gain for the most people, and minimal pain for as few as possible. Do more for more, with less pain for fewer. We practice wisdom by looking at *how* we are thinking and *where* we have been looking, and if we have missed anything.

There are three principles in mastering our thoughts and practising wisdom:

1. *Adaption:* Find the best way. This is not a solo activity! We need to undertake creative activities to generate novel ideas. We need to collaborate with others to elicit contrasting views, deeper insights, and richer perspectives. We then need to cooperate to implement new changes.

2. *Synthesis:* Find the best idea. This is trickier than it looks! It means including as many perspectives as possible. Select the best aspects of each. Integrate these into a new way forward

3. *Oscillation:* Find the best balance. Everything is a polarity; what looks like an opposite but is really complementary. Some examples: give and take, consume and create, effort and rest.

With these three principles in hand, we are ready to really challenge our thinking. On the road to wise decision-making, we must be rigorous and thorough. A checking process is outlined next.

Decision-making filters

EXTEND – applying wisdom to sense making

- Questions: What questions are we asking? What other questions could we be asking? What questions are we avoiding asking? What question would a ten-year-old ask? What questions would our 100-year-old self ask?

- Patterns: What patterns of results or behaviour have we been seeing? For how long? How predictable are they? How repeatable are they?

- Systems: Which systems have we mapped? What other systems could we map? Have we looked at the underpinning worldviews? Have we looked at the values guiding our point of view?

- Points of view: How much diversity do we have in our perspectives? Diversity includes: gender, gender identity, sexual preference, behaviour preferences, age, religion, cultural background, cognitive processing, thinking preferences, and economic situation. What would the wisest people we know, or know from history, do or say about this?

- Lived experience: Have we consulted our lived experience with this decision? Have we looked at others' lived experience? Have other organisations faced similar things and what have they done with what results?

DISTIL – applying wisdom to making sense

- Values: Have we established what our values are, individually and collectively? Have we ranked our guiding values before making this decision? Does this choice fit with our values?

- Assumptions: What are we assuming to be true? What if these are not true?

- Evidence: What evidence are we using to help make this decision? How credible is this evidence? Based on what criteria?

- Repercussions: Who will this affect the most, for better and worse? What are the positive side effects of this decision? What could be some unintended consequences? What if we did nothing – what would be the impact? What if we did the opposite – what impact would that have?

- Decision-making process: How did we arrive at this decision? Did everyone have an opportunity to think independently first? Have we explored all the ideas offered? What was the criteria for our decision? What was the process for the decision: democratic? Consultative? Unilateral? What is our gut instinct telling us? What are our emotions telling us?

- Ethics: Does this value fit with our ethical framework? Can we live with all the consequences of this decision? Can we live with this choice if we are wrong?

In endeavouring to act with wisdom, we need to reassure ourselves that we have done everything we can with what we know at the time. This helps us to know we have considered the choices from the broadest, most thorough lens possible, given what we know of ourselves and the situation.

When we consider the situation with Karen and Frank, it's easy to jump to the conclusion that this is a personality problem. In doing the work of expanding and focusing our point of view, then considering our options by applying the lens of wisdom, we can arrive at very different conclusions. We can see that some of the structures of the organisation are leading to outcomes that do not support the values we aspire to. The problem is not necessarily people, but systems. The wisdom lens helps us to slow down and be sensible in our approach. We can avoid burning people unnecessarily, and we can work to strengthen systems and relationships instead.

Ultimately wisdom comes from knowing we know nothing. This keeps us humble and out of the hubris trap, and is what numerous luminaries throughout history have asserted:

> *"The fool doth think he is wise, but the wise
> man knows himself to be a fool."*
> – As You Like It, William Shakespeare

> *"The only true wisdom is in knowing you know nothing."*
> – Socrates

> *"We can know only that we know nothing. And that
> is the highest degree of human wisdom."*
> – War and Peace, Leo Tolstoy

> *"The more I read, the more I acquire, the more
> certain I am that I know nothing."*
> – Voltaire

At this stage, we have expanded our perspective as broadly as possible, then refined it through various focus filters, then calibrated it by testing our thinking itself. By this stage, we know that we have done the best we can, given what we know. We also need to make sure we are acting with compassion. We need to balance the best of our mind with the best of our heart.

4. Mastering feelings, or the art of being sensitive and compassionate

In this final quadrant in Figure 1 (see page 19), we ask ourselves: What is compassion? At its core, compassion is a deep understanding and concern for the suffering of others and a strong desire to alleviate their suffering. It's distinct from empathy. Empathy is feeling what others are feeling: if you feel sad, I feel sad too. Empathy is important because it helps us to build rapport and care for each other.

Empathy can lead us off-track. Neuroscience and psychology show that we have the most empathy towards those we find attractive and who seem similar to us. We might be called to act more on behalf of those who look like, sound like, and live like us, than those who do not. If we think about the Frank and Karen case, our empathy for one or the other can skew our choices when it comes to resolving the issue. So, we must endeavour to move beyond our empathy and use compassion to balance our choices.

It is compassion that moves us beyond empathy, because we see and acknowledge suffering in all living things, not just those who belong to our 'tribe'. Then we feel compelled to alleviate it if we can.

There are three principles for compassionate action:

1. *Compassion includes others.* When we expand our thinking as far as possible into the future and past, as wide as possible across countries and lands, then we are able to include more and more of humanity, place, and planet. Compassion has no limits of geography or temporal limitations.

2. *Compassion elevates others.* When we consider our choices, we ask ourselves, will it uplift all of us in the implementation?

3. *Ask: What would love do?* This is the highest form of kindness. If we are making tough decisions, this filter steadies our hand and helps make the bad bearable.

> **Decision-making filters**
>
> *INCLUDE: Applying compassion to sense-making*
>
> In our choosing, have we considered the far-ranging impacts on others? Even those we may never meet, like generations to come, or a child living on the streets in a foreign land.
>
> *DISCERN: Applying compassion to making sense*
>
> Will this choice uplift humanity or bring out its worst?
>
> Is this choice kind?
>
> If it is not kind, can we show deep kindness and care in the execution of the choice?

When compassion is included in our perspective of expansion, we include more and more stakeholders. We consider the effects of our choices for the widest possible circle. When we apply compassion to our focus lens, we determine how we can best elevate those who are in our circle of influence.

When thinking about Karen and Frank, we can choose to be compassionate towards both of them. Both mean well, both are motivated to perform. We can feel compassion for Frank who is struggling to fulfil his work ambitions, and we can express compassion for Karen who feels she is being held back and disrespected. When we balance this with wisdom, we can arrive at practical and uplifting solutions.

Compassion involves finding the balance between sensible and sensitive.

In the case with Frank and Karen, wise action consists in amending the systems that are driving divisive behaviour, such as the remuneration formula. It would also include collaborative discussions around resource allocation and collective problem solving that could help all staff progress. Compassionate action consists of acknowledging Frank's financial strain while also encouraging Karen's healthy ambition. By discussing these situations openly, conflict is diminished and the opportunity for cooperation is opened.

Humility and care swings us between sensitive and sensible. It reminds us that ultimately we know nothing, though we try our best. It reminds us that we are everything, and our actions affect us all, big and small.

What affects our perspective

Layers in communication

There is what people say, and then there is what they mean. In previous processes like the problem tree, we have endeavoured to explore the roots of problems. We dig under the surface to see what is causing the behaviour and interactions that are problematic.

According to Church, Stein and Henderson in their book *Thought Leaders* (2011), communication and miscommunication is the core of developing perspective. In their model, there are three levels of communication:

1. Content: What is being said.
2. Concept: What we are making that mean, our interpretation of the event/s.
3. Context: The bigger picture of what we feel this is really about.

Because of our different meaning-making machinery, we can participate in the same event, yet have vastly different interpretations and significance around the incident. Let's apply their model to see what we uncover with Karen and Frank:

> **"He's mean." "She's selfish."**
>
> Let's tease out their different perspectives:
>
> For Karen, it might be something like:
>
> Content: "Frank is trying to steal my staff again."
>
> Concept: "He is jealous and doesn't want to see me get ahead of him."
>
> Context: "This is about respect."
>
> For Frank, it might be something like:
>
> Content: "Karen is blocking me again."
>
> Concept: "She is selfish and greedy – she just wants to get ahead in spite of everyone else."
>
> Context: "This is about being a team player".
>
> When we start to play with the lenses of perspective, we start to troubleshoot these crossed wires and get to the heart of what matters for all parties. The simple interpretation is not often the best or correct one. As the leader in this situation, we can start to unpack the issues with each of them by digging into the story they are telling about the situation. We want to get to the context lens they are looking through.

Leadership maturity and perspective

We have to be at a certain stage of leadership maturity to practise perspective with wisdom and compassion. Various integral leadership models map worldviews, values, and action logics on a development scale. The scales are ever-expanding and ever more inclusive. What's important to us and who is important to us expands as our worldview expands. In earlier stages, our main concerns are selfish: how do I survive? As we become more mature, socially competent and integrated (assuming our context is conducive to this), we start to care and focus more on others, and ask: how do I fit into a group, and how will the group survive and thrive? As we mature as leaders and challenge our perspective, our sense of 'group' gets bigger and bigger.

Let's look briefly at each of the stages as mapped out by Bill Torbert and associates in *Action Logic – The secret of timely and transforming leadership* (2004).

The Opportunist stage. The opportunist stage of development is a survival one. We feel that it is us against the world. We seek to win and get ahead. Its gift is assertiveness. Its challenge is selfishness. We can see both Frank and Karen acting through this lens.

The Diplomat stage. When we move beyond immediate self-interest, we discover the value of being part of a group, team and tribe. Following the rules and fitting in is important for social harmony and stability. Karen's inner Diplomat is rattled when Frank appears to be stealing both staff and opportunities. She cries, "it's not fair". For Frank, he believes that it is Karen who is not following the rules; she is not being a team player and sharing access and resources.

The Expert stage. When we feel comfortable in a group and we build our expertise, we develop the will and desire to stand out and be recognised. We feel that our experience is valuable and our opinion, based on our experience and expertise, ought to be considered. We learn how to speak up and speak out. In our scenario, Karen is seeking to deepen her expertise and that of the team. Speaking up is challenging for her and she has done so privately with her supervisor.

She is moving into matters of the Expert stage, but is possibly not quite there yet.

The Achiever stage. When we start to work in teams, we realise the value of working together to create better outcomes faster than we could on our own. Karen is well aware of this as she works on building her team's capacity. Frank is also well aware of this as he seeks to bolster his team's resources. He knows that not having a fully functional team is affecting his team results as well as his personal ones. Neither has quite seen how their actions as colleagues are affecting the outcomes for the broader organisation. Their perspective is firmly on their own team and their own outcomes, rather than broadly across teams. This is how silos emerge and are embedded in organisations.

The Individualist stage. When we start to realise that each of us have a point of view and that each of us have rich experiences to share, then we are able to expand perspective enormously. We get curious about systems and points of view. We look for diversity of thought and experience as a way of enriching the whole. Neither Frank nor Karen are here yet. As leaders, if we are to resolve these issues well, we must be. This is where the practice of perspective really comes to the fore and needs to be mastered.

The Strategist stage. When we reach this stage, we look at the interactive systems in an organisation and beyond that contribute to the problems faced by Karen and Frank. When we are at this stage we fully exercise the practice of perspective: zooming out to see time, complexity, and meaning; and zooming in to see scenarios, problem trees, and challenging assumptions. We balance wise decisions with compassionate choices. This is well beyond Frank and Karen's experience and context. As leaders, we want to be at Strategist stage if we are going to make the best decisions not only for Frank and Karen, but for their teams, the organisation, the stakeholders it serves, and the broader community.

Depending on our progress as a leader, we may have a different context for expanding our perspective. Earlier stages of leadership maturity constrain our circle of concern to more immediate spheres. If we are at an earlier stage such as the Diplomat, then our primary concern for survival is fitting in. Being part of a group is our core objective and sense of safety and identity. In order to be part of an 'in' group, sometimes we need to be apart from a group. When we are Diplomat stage, belonging is core to our motivation. This need to belong never leaves us. The size and scope of the group however does shift and become much bigger as we expand our ability to see and be in the world. The skills at the Diplomat stage are about fitting in, following the rules, and being a positive social citizen, according to the laws of the group with which we identify. These are useful skills that ensure civilised and collaborative experiences.

These skills do have limitations, however. We tend to be black and white in our thinking: either we follow the rules and fit in, or don't follow the rules and must be punished. Later stages of leadership maturity can consider the soft edges of rules and how they are contextual and sometimes serve and sometimes don't. For example, if not killing someone is a rule, how then do we allow for protecting oneself against harm if that person is threatening our lives? Do we punish the person who would have been killed had they not acted defensively?

These blurry edges are the capacities of later stages of leadership maturity when we no longer identify our sense of ego and identity with fitting in, but with something different. At Expert stage, we attach our identity to expertise and experience: how much I know and have experienced determines my self-worth. We judge others according to the same criteria: how much do they know and are trained in? What is their body of expertise and is it sufficient to be considered worthwhile listening to? The Achiever filters much of their perspective through the lens of: "will this make it easier or better? Will this help us produce better results faster?"

From the Individualist onwards, wisdom and compassion come fully into play. As soon as we start to map the systems that underpin a visible problem, we know we are approaching the realm of practising a broader perspective and have a chance of exercising both wisdom and compassion. If we see the Frank and Karen problem as simply a personality problem, then we know there is work to be done in developing our perspective.

Other factors that affect our perspective

Physical sensations and restrictions

When we are in pain, it is difficult to elevate our focus beyond our immediate needs. The body is our physical vehicle for perspective, and sometimes it is not always the most optimal lens. If we are tall, we see the world differently. I once sat behind a very tall man on a long flight to Bali. His legs were so long that even in splaying his knees wide apart, they pressed painfully into the seat in front of him. His head towered above the headrest making it an uncomfortable block pressing into the back of his neck. He could only lean forward with his arms crossed on the back of the chair in front to get some reprieve. For him, flying is a painful experience. Planes are not built with his context in mind: they are built to fit 'average'. This is where we can be blind to perspective. What is 'average'? An average man? An average woman? In which culture or country? These are things that can hamper our perspective.

Cognitive bias

We are skewed to see the world based on our own experience. Something is either good or bad relative to our previous patterns of experiences. Until we start practising perspective and challenging our assumptions, we do not see these blindspots and we operate by default.

Perspective is power. When we can see and feel more, we can respond with ever more savvy and service. When we can see both like an ant and an eagle, then we will know more of the earth.

BRASS TACKS

Practising perspective

I worried about this chapter being too broad and theoretical in scope. After all, if you are struggling with Frank and Karen and their ongoing turf wars, it seems a stretch to consider generations into the future and past and all the systems at play that may contribute to this challenge.

And that's my point. What looks like simple challenges are deep and complex human concerns. If we don't consider the Frank and Karen problem as a problem for humanity, we can exercise neither wisdom nor compassion. So, using the model of practicing perspective at the start of this section, let's get down to brass tacks:

Practise sense making

Make it a regular practice to do an environmental scan (regular meaning monthly). Incorporate daily awareness habits to scan the horizon and see what is going on. Use curation tools to do this: I use the app Flipboard, Google Alerts (see www.google.com/alerts) and the newsletter Shaping Tomorrow (see www.shapingtomorrow.com/) to curate information on trends to which I am paying the most attention.

Practise making sense

Undertake regular scenario planning to complement your strategic review. Once a year is too infrequent. Quarterly is likely a good cadence. Consider what is happening – if volatility is increasing, consider undertaking some scenario planning ahead of this regular interval.

Act with wisdom: Be sensible

Consider all your choices and actions through the filters of wisdom, remembering you know nothing.

Act with compassion: Be sensitive

Consider all your choices through the filter of 'what would love do? Taking things at face value is never the right thing to do. Humans are messy creatures with a jumble of perspectives and experiences that drive our interactions and choices. We can however use different maps to help navigate this convoluted wilderness.

Now that we've explored our point of view from all sorts of wide and deep angles, it's time to look somewhere even more challenging: at ourselves.

PART THREE

YOU

Perspective on self

One of the most important aspects of the practice of perspective is becoming mindful of how we see ourselves as leaders. It's not often that we pause and ask: 'how I am showing up right now? Am I having the impact I want?' When we get intentional about how we see ourselves and what role we play, then we can amplify our impact enormously. In this section, we take a look at particular archetypes that can guide our action for more powerful results.

BOARDROOM CASE STUDY

The pied piper

Jennifer looked despondent. It had been another tough week.

"I am sick of the battle. Every time I go into an executive meeting, I feel like I'm fighting uphill all the way. They don't get it. I just can't get them to listen."

She had been advocating for changes to basic business processes she saw as fundamental requirements to safe practices. Her colleagues were skeptical at best, stonewalling at worst.

"I feel like a crusader in an urgent war the others don't even know we're in! We're all going to come unstuck if we don't fix this."

"How does it feel to be a 'Crusader'?" I asked.

"Lonely. Dangerous. Exhausting. Maybe even a little pointless."

"Is there a different role you might play? One that isn't so confrontational or focused on battles?"

Jennifer sat back and paused.

"Hmm. I wonder if I could do it better with a softly, softly approach. More of a pied piper."

"That's different! How does that feel?"

"It's a different kind of challenge. I'll need to be more clever and concerted in my efforts. You know what though, it feels a bit more fun!"

Jennifer changed her approach. Instead of heady arguments about why they must do something and how perilous it was if they didn't, and berating colleagues for no sense of urgency, she softened her language. She used suggestions. She used stories. She invited opinions. She asked questions of others about their priorities. She shaped her recommendations to resonate with her colleagues' biggest concerns. Bit by bit, she got her safety agenda changes implemented. She had to rein in her 'charge ahead' energy and timeline in favour of a more measured approach, but she got the job done.

I asked a number of leaders what analogy they would use to describe their role as a leader. Here is a sample of responses:

"I am like a traffic control cop. I am constantly directing where to go, what to do and how to do it. If I had a whistle that would be perfect!"

"I feel like a referee. I'm constantly keeping the warring factions apart and trying to settle disputes."

"I'm a gardener. Each of the plants needs a different amount of water and attention. Together they form a wonderful landscape."

"I'm definitely a coach. I try to get the best out of my people. Help them to learn for themselves. I help build more leaders this way."

"I'm a parent, that's for sure! They need a lot of support and handholding. Young people don't seem to have too much resilience these days."

"I'm a lighthouse. I am showing the way."

How we see ourselves as leaders shapes our attitude and actions. Sometimes these personas are useful, sometimes they work against what we are trying to achieve. Sometimes they inspire us, sometimes they exhaust us.

What's important is that we are intentional about what story we choose to guide our decisions and interactions. Most of the time we choose a role in reaction to our experience, based on our emotional reactions to situations. We are letting circumstance dictate our feelings and our demeanour.

What we want is to be deliberate in our lens of how we see ourselves. The best way to do this is through archetypes.

BIG PICTURE

Working towards your perspective on self

Archetypes are universal roles or patterns of behaviour that resonate across cultures. They are a blueprint for a story arc and narrative. We understand the tone and purpose of an archetypal journey and can see ourselves fulfilling that function.

Archetypes create the architecture for action. The patterns of the story help shape our decisions and actions.

When we think of the Hero archetype, what do we think of? We think of a reluctant brave soul called to solve a difficult challenge for a purpose greater than themselves. We know the hero must be brave, face brutal challenges, and ultimately triumph. It's a core story pattern that is so fundamental to the human experience, we recognise it across cultures. This is the work Joseph Campbell did in *The Hero with a Thousand Faces* (1949).

Lesser known is the work of his student, Maureen Murdock who tracked the Heroine's story in her book, *The Heroine's Journey: Woman's Quest for Wholeness* (1990). While the Hero's journey is about an external journey of conquest, the heroine's is an internal one. She learns to trust herself and be courageous. The Hero's journey is about developing strength and power in the external world, while the Heroine's is about strength and power in the inner world.

In *Composure – How centered leaders make the biggest impact* (2015), I outlined the male and female archetypes to integrate in our personal leadership journey. And now, in *People Stuff*, I help business leaders look at archetypes through the lens of business outcomes and choose relevant ones accordingly. Throughout my research and experience, I have found that there are two main frames for business leadership: purpose and ethos.

I define purpose as what we collectively want to achieve through the business or organisation. In purpose, business outcomes swing between two tensions: to build and to win. I define ethos as the values that underpin our core concerns. In ethos, the tension travels between the values to protect and to progress.

Four main archetypes emerge as we match these tensions:

The Diplomat whose purpose is to win and values are to progress.

The Warrior whose purpose is to win and values are to protect.

The Guardian whose purpose is to build and values are to protect.

The Pioneer whose purpose is to build and values are to progress.

There is a fifth archetype which acts as an amplifier for each of these four: the Elder. The Elder exercises leadership through the most expanded version of the perspective lens. They extend perspective as far as they can into the future and past, and then drill down to the current moment. Then they take action with wisdom and compassion. The Elder is both sensible and sensitive. As an overlay for the other archetypes, the Elder helps keep us from falling into the Shadow Archetypes.

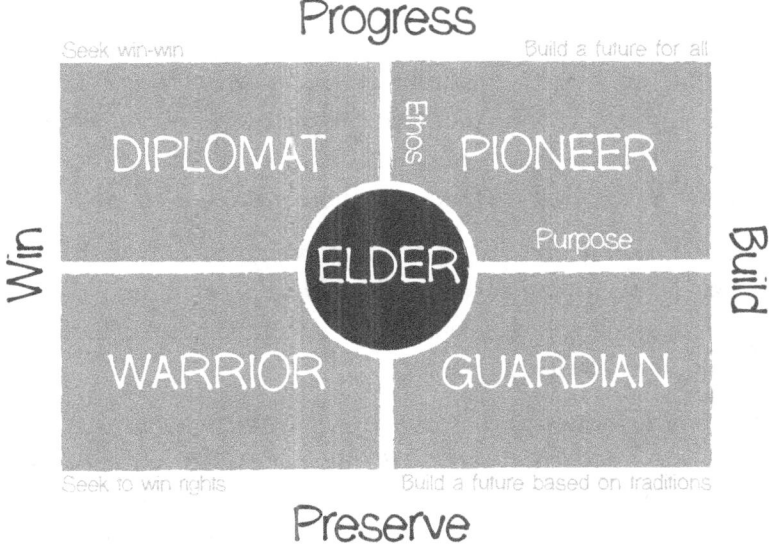

Figure 5: The five archetypes

Each archetype has its pitfalls and strengths, including the Elder. In exploring these profiles, we must highlight how to avoid the pitfalls, which are the Shadow Archetypes. We also want to highlight the context for which each profile is appropriate and useful.

About archetypes[9]

Archetypes have existed in various cultures across the ages. In Roman, Greek and many other cultures, we called them gods and goddesses. Archetypes form a template or a guide to human behaviour, both good and bad. They provide a form or a pattern to which we can aspire or avoid. They serve to inform us about our motivations and desired outcomes. They are blueprints for what is possible for us. Psychiatrist Carl Jung is famous for making us aware of archetypes. He saw archetypes as the fundamental units of the human mind. These units are forms or images or patterns that show up in ancient religions, myths, legends, and fairytales.

---

9   In researching this part of the book I found a treasure trove of information on archetypes here: www.scottjeffrey.com/archetypes-psychology. More books in Resources at the back. Knock yourself out.

We see archetypes in stories and movies. We can think of them as the roles that we play in our lives. This is the more familiar application of archetypes. These types of roles include mother, caregiver, parent, mentor, and coach. They are powerful sources of energy behind our behaviour. They are secret codes that can imprint on our consciousness and subconsciousness to direct our choices and our actions.

I first wrote about archetypes in *Composure* to encourage the reader to make deliberate choices about the archetypes that can guide their experience as a leader. I encourage the mindful choice of archetypes that embrace polarities.

I have long advocated the selection of one word or archetype to guide one's choices for a period of time. Be that for 90 days, a year, or longer. As I wrote this book, the archetype I picked was Luminary. I chose this one in particular because it reminds me to be visible, to be a guide, to be a spokesperson. It helps remind me to get my message out into the world and that my own petty fears are nothing in the face of the purpose of the Luminary.

Archetypes influence behaviour. They are patterns we can adopt and choose to act upon. If we see ourselves as an adventurer for example, the archetype of the Adventurer will infuse our consciousness and mould our choices. On a day-to-day basis as an Adventurer, we might choose to reach out to people we don't know, to make sales calls we wouldn't otherwise make, and say yes to opportunities we would otherwise say no to. Archetypes can guide us into new experiences that we might not otherwise have chosen.

Archetypes can also trigger emotions. Different archetypes are associated with different emotional experiences. The Warrior is courageous. The Guardian is dedicated. The Diplomat is stoic. The Pioneer is adventurous. The Elder is calm. Archetypes can also give us a sense of purpose and meaning. In this book, I've selected specific archetypes distributed according to business purpose. While I propose five essential archetypes here, there are an infinite number of archetypes we could select to help shape our leadership.

About shadow work

In each of our intentions, there exists potential for the negative. We may have noble intentions that go sour, often due to a narrowing of perspective.

All of us have shadows within us. All of us have the potential for great good, great ethics and great contribution. The shadow side is the potential for the opposite. Where we have love, we also have hate. Where we have calm, rage. That is because our emotions exist on a spectrum: where there is light, there is shadow. The *Star Wars* series captured this perfectly with the dark side of the Force versus the light side of the Force. We're always having to choose between the two. We don't ever destroy one, we try to bring balance.

We can't rid ourselves of shadow. We can suppress it and we can ignore it – but the worst part is when we fail to see it. This flaw is rife in leadership. Somebody might believe themselves to be a warrior, when they have in fact turned bully. They may see themselves as a wise leader when in fact they are a tyrant. They may see themselves as a master diplomat, but are really a manipulator. They may see themselves as guardians of the just and the good. In reality, they have become a fanatic.

From an early age we are encouraged to nurture our good traits and disassociate the bad traits. Greed, envy and jealousy are seen as bad, whereas being nice, generous and supportive are seen as good. So we are constantly judging ourselves, our shadow and our light, even though they're all integral aspects of ourselves. The repression of all these bundled up parts of ourselves becomes our baggage. We drag it around with us and it can become a real impediment to good leadership.

In Carl Jung's work in psychology, he describes the shadow as an unconscious part of our personality. It often consists of the negative aspects of ourselves we would deny or disown. When we bury parts of ourselves we have labeled as bad, we project these traits on others as a way of processing the negative charge around it. We project onto others what we want to deny in ourselves. This is one of the reasons why we find some people irritating. If we don't like the way that people are behaving, chances are, we have that behaviour buried deep in us. If we don't like rude people or we don't like jealous or small-minded people, then there's an aspect of ourselves that we have not come to terms with. We judge others for these negative traits, because we haven't done the conscious work on ourselves. So, we project it onto others and judge others for being bad people with bad traits.

Whether you agree with the Jungian theory of projection or not, it's a useful frame for self-examination.

Remember the dog poo incident? As I sit judging my neighbours, I ask, "where am I being selfish and sly?" As I reflect on some of my own poor behaviours, including not picking up dog poo in a nature reserve when I was minding the neighbour's dog, I am struck by my own hypocrisy. I am the very thing I was judging my neighbours for. I realise I have been the pot calling the kettle black.

The good news is, when we start to explore our shadow self and pay attention to it, we are not triggered as easily. Paradoxically, we become less judgmental. We become more compassionate, because we see every human as a flawed human, just like ourselves. All of us have the bully, the manipulator, the fanatic, the gambler, and the tyrant within us.

The sooner we can see that we have the capacity for this, the easier it is to reconcile and become more in line with our light side. When we practice self-compassion for all the negative aspects of ourselves, we can let go of shame and guilt. We take an honest look at our attitudes, our behaviours, and our dark thoughts, then we take them out of the driver's seat. We can just notice them and let them be.

What can we do to avoid our shadow? The first point is not to avoid it. If you've ever caught yourself thinking something absolutely horrendous, just make note of it. It's just a thought. It's just your shadow side. It doesn't have to be made manifest. The second point is to explore it. One exercise is to make note of when you are emotionally triggered. If you find yourself judging or reacting to somebody else's behaviour, make note of that behaviour. Then ask yourself, when are you expressing that behaviour? When are you a tyrant? When are you a manipulator?

In projection, we see in others what we deny in ourselves. If we see in others something we dislike, just put up the mirror and have a look. Another exercise is to make a list of all your good traits on one side of the page. On the opposite page, identify its negative opposite. Then explore where you have those behaviours and those traits.

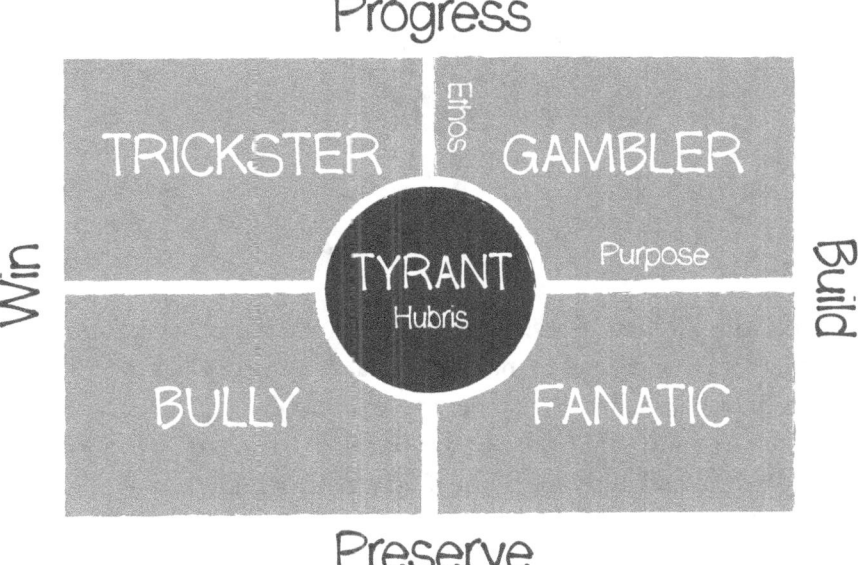

Figure 6: Shadows of the five main archetypes

In the following sections we'll take a deeper dive into each of the leadership archetypes, and what pulls us to the dark side of each one. Our core objective is to raise our awareness and perspective on what we are capable of, and choose a positive path.

The five archetypes

Archetype 1: The Elder

The Elder Archetype is the amplifier of all the other leadership archetypes. It is central to making wise and compassionate decisions, regardless of which other archetype we choose as a primary one for the situation. In other words, pay attention! This part is important. Plus, we kick off with one of the most amazing leaders on the global stage, Mary Robinson.

BOARDROOM CASE STUDY

"We are all in this together"
– Mary Robinson

Mary Robinson is a total leadership badass. She can smell a fight for justice a mile away. She's like an Avenger in a business suit. Her badassery was honed at an early age as she was the only girl between two sets of brothers. She had to fight tooth and nail to hold her own. She says it sparked her interest in human rights early.

Later she studied as a lawyer and was eventually elected as the first female President of Ireland, from 1990 to 1997.

Fighting for what was fair and equitable was the drumbeat of Robinson's leadership passion. To this she added the chorus 'no one should be left behind and 'we are all in this together'. This song shaped her thinking and eventually her political agenda. In her subsequent roles at the United Nations as High Commissioner for Human Rights, and then in the establishment of her own foundation named the Mary Robinson Foundation for Climate Justice, she led projects to advocate and promote human rights for all.

Through her Foundation, she makes the link that climate action is the biggest threat to human rights.[10] She states it's the most vulnerable nations that will suffer the most in climate change. Small island nations with few resources will watch the sea rise and swallow their lands. They are likely to be dispossessed, with their homeland underwater. Climate refugees.

Robinson is currently chair of the Elders group and sits on the B Team alongside Sir Richard Branson. She also wrote a book called *Everyone Matters* (2012). This is a poignant summary of her leadership philosophy and approach: we are all in this together, and we need to look after each other. She works across business, politics, climate change, and social justice as interconnected systems that need to be integrated well in order to support thriving successfully in harmony with our planet and its resources. She believes it's possible if we are committed and follow through.

BIG PICTURE

The Elder Archetype

The Elder is the embodiment of wisdom and compassion. It is central to the five Archetypes model as it represents the broadest and most evolved perspective. We can rise above factionalism and political agendas to seek the highest good for all. We want to channel the essence of the Elder through the other archetypes so we can access their highest form. For example, we can channel Warrior, and infuse it with an Elder flavour. This ensures our Warrior efforts are altruistic and unblinkered.

---

10 Watch her TED talk on climate change and its impact on human rights on YouTube.

We can invoke the archetype of the Elder in both stable conditions and in crisis. 'Let cooler heads prevail' is one of the mantras of Elders. The Elder Archetype serves us best when we need to make difficult decisions in complex circumstances. When there is a lot at stake, for us, for others, for the broader stakeholders and community, then the Elder is our best ally.

In literature and myths, the Elder appears as the Sage or the Crone. They are venerated for wisdom and sound judgment. They are held to have insight beyond regular experiences, based on a long life of experience and reflective practice.

In North American First Nations people, Elders hold an important and respected role. They are keepers of tribal knowledge and cultural practices. Their role is to share wisdom, not teach it. They are seen as wisdom keepers and are consulted on matters that are of importance to the tribe more broadly, as well as to moderate in difficult situations.

For Australian Aboriginal people, an Elder is someone who is acknowledged as a custodian of wisdom and lore, and who has permission to disclose knowledge and beliefs. They may also have specific responsibilities such as performing Welcome to Country ceremonies or greetings at formal functions where there are visitors from other lands.

In any culture however, age alone does not qualify one as an Elder. Age does not automatically make us wise. Being an Elder is about having and sharing wisdom while being respected. Elder leaders seek the best solution for as many as possible. We cultivate 'people first' cultures. Our sense of inclusion is vast. We are constantly seeking to make a long-term contribution and solve long-term issues. We see this approach in a number of organisations and businesses operating globally.

One of the most inspiring organisations is The Elders, which was founded by Nelson Mandela in 2007.[11] Their manifesto reads: "the Elders are an independent group of global leaders working together for peace, justice and human rights. Our vision is of a world where

---

11   Check them out here: www.theelders.org/

people live in peace, conscious of their common humanity and their shared responsibilities for each other, for the planet and for future generations. We envisage a world in which there is universal respect for human rights; in which poverty has been eliminated; in which people are free from fear and oppression and are able to fulfil their true potential."

International non-profit organisation The B-Team[12], co-founded by Richard Branson and Jochen Zeitz in 2012, is based on their mutual belief that business can, and must, be a driving force for social, environmental and economic benefit. The focus of the B Team is for business to lead the way to improving climate outcomes and management, work towards workplace equality, and advocate for better business governance.

Traits and style of the Elder Archetype

As an Elder, we need to hold lightly our insights, experience, and judgment, knowing they have value, while also exploring and finding solutions in a collaborative way. In doing so, we are largely guided by the traits of humility, curiosity and care.

Humility: Elders are humbled by experience, not inflated by it. Experience is one of our most valuable assets, if we have learned from it. Experience should teach us that the more we know, the less we know, and the more there is to know.

Curiosity: Curiosity is the cure for arrogance. When we are curious, it leaves us open to new insights and learning. Arrogance deflects learning. When we are arrogant, we think we know best. It blinds us to other opinions and perspectives.

Care: Care is the default intention of an Elder. The Elder cares about the listener, about the impact, about their message. Harmony and peace is our ultimate aspiration and intention. We take care with our words, take care with our relationships, and take care of how we show up and engage.

---

12   The B Team is at bteam.org/

> While we are guided by these three traits, we also seek to share wisdom. It is a polarity: to express wisdom and insight and sound judgment while also being curious and humble. The approach is Socratic and collaborative, preferring to lead reflection with questions rather than answers.

Cultures created by the Elder Archetype

Elders navigate the polarities and paradox of culture. They acknowledge both the need for group identity and the value of belonging, and for having a cause that is unique and important to the people within that community, be it a group, business, club, or association. At the same time, Elders foster an 'Only Us' ethos. The Us is defined very broadly: all sentient beings and the planet on which we live. Though we might unite as a sub-section of humanity, ultimately we all belong to one thing: existence. Our circle of concern and care is the widest possible. As such, the cultures we lead and create are compassionate and caring ones. We endeavour to navigate between self-interest and the greater good with grace and wisdom.

People stuff issues still arise in cultures led by Elders. These can include disillusionment when others do not operate by the same high standards. We can also be subject to the same primal challenges: jealousy, belonging, recognition. Elders have shadow within too.

Elders are seekers of Truth, Beauty, and Goodness. These are the foremost anchors in our approach. These are known as the Transcendentals and pertain to the three aspects of the human field of interest and their ideals. Read another way, Truth is science, Beauty is the arts, and Goodness is religion or spirituality. Read yet another way, this is the focus of head, heart, and hands.

As Elders, our sense of time is expansive. We look to multiple generations in the past and multiple generations to the future. Australian First Nations cultures have a huge sense of connection to ancestors. They have responsibility to honour those that came before and cherish their land and practices for generations to come. It's one of the reasons that many place names in Aboriginal languages are descriptive of the landscape (for example Larapinta, a special place in the desert outside of Alice Springs, means salty water; there is also a pass called Inarlanga Pass, or echidna pass). Rarely are landscape features or place names named after living or dead people. This does not make sense in the Australian Aboriginal paradigm; they see people's role as custodians passing through while the land and nature endures.

The Great Law of the Iroquois embodies this notion in their Seven Generations principle. They believe that every decision we make, and every action, must be considered for its impact on seven generations down the line, or roughly two hundred years from now.

When we consider who are stakeholders from an Elders point of view, our considerations get broader and more noble.

Elder beliefs and practices

Ask. Asking guarantees humility and curiosity. When we ask, we admit we can't do it on our own and that we don't know enough by ourselves. Asking keeps our attention out and focused on others.

Learn. When we focus on what we can learn, we keep our sensors open and our perspective flexible.

Share. Leaders learn best when they share what they have learned. It helps consolidate and apply the insights in real time.

Circles, not triangles. Consultation and collaboration strengthens engagement.

Principles sustain. Leadership is a tough gig. What can keep someone going through insurmountable challenges? Fundamental beliefs in the cause, and one that puts people and peace first.

Every leader operates within a system. Changing it means you need to be able to see the system and the values that underpin it. Changing the system ultimately means changing these values. This is a longer value proposition than simply introducing a new program.

To change a system, we still need to operate within it. If a fish notices the water in their pond is cloudy, they still need to swim in it. Campaigning within a system means there are still constraints.

People will campaign against ethical change if their own self interests are at stake. We saw this in all big social reforms like slavery and segregation. Appealing to people's higher nature did not always win over opponents if it meant privilege and benefits were at stake.

Sometimes we cannot live up to our own moral standards because we are constrained by the system in which we find ourselves. Barack Obama wanted to dismantle Guantanamo Bay and found when he was in office, he couldn't.

Being an Elder and building a 'people first' culture, may mean a long campaign of winning hearts and minds. It may mean that our values and actions may not always line up as cleanly as we intended.

The Elder's shadow: The Tyrant

If we are as wise and compassionate as an Elder, how then do we succumb to shadow? It starts with hubris. We might pause to assess our accomplishments and feel a surge of pride. This is a wonderful feeling and so our attention is drawn to our own concerns. This is where the downward slide starts.

Once we realise how much status we have gained and how fabulous the privileges of authority are, then we start to fear their loss. In his book *The Power Paradox* (2016), Dr Dacher Keltner makes the critical observation that power is granted by followers, not taken from them. The book investigates how power is given for the small acts that bind people together and create greater benefits for the group. When we undertake small actions that encourage and uplift others and generate good outcomes for the group, then we are rewarded with the privileges of power: status, esteem, and the giddy surge of dopamine in the brain that comes from making a contribution to the world. Enthusiasm, inspiration and hope spark the dopamine floods. Dopamine is a feel-good neurotransmitter and is incredibly addictive. It's what gets triggered when we find something that was lost or when we complete a task. It's the neurotransmitter that gets fired up when gambling, playing online games and doing emails.

That feel-good dopamine switch can turn Elders into Tyrants.

Dr Keltner observes: "When we are feeling powerful, our actions become more self-focused rather than focused on the greater good … When we are feeling powerful, we are moved more by our own experiences than those of other people … experiences of power and privilege are a like a form of brain damage, leading us to self-serving, impulsive behaviour."

Let's look at the Elder and its shadow, the Tyrant:

Elder	Tyrant
Humility	Hubris
Greater good	Greater status
Collaborative	Unilateral
Compassionate	Dispassionate
Uplifts others	Uses others

The shift to Tyrant begins with **hubris**. When we allow arrogance to rise, we become more focused on ourselves and we lose ourselves, sliding into the shadow.

It started so well – Adam Neumann of WeWork

There is no more public example of the Elder to Tyrant arc than Adam Neumann, founder of co-working space WeWork. WeWork was founded with the purpose to elevate the world's consciousness through belonging and togetherness. Neumann's creation of funky, collective workspaces for gig economy workers and soloists was a shining light for collectivism and community. It was altruism and capitalism all rolled into one. It's an Elder's vision made glorious by a charismatic leader. We bestow power on individuals like Neumann who show enthusiasm and lead actions for the greater good. Sometimes this goes wrong.

In less than a decade, WeWork grew from two locations to properties around the globe with some 12,500 employees. They expanded the concept of leveraging communal resources and launched initiatives like WeLive, (short-term communal dorms), Rise by We (fitness facilities) and WeGrow (experiential learning primary school).

WeWork was the poster-child for a new way of working: the Gig economy and its pioneering independent soloist startup entrepreneurs thriving together, working independently, in community-oriented spaces.

Neumann's success groomed his hubris. He showed every excess warned about in the 'Abuses of Power' chapter in *The Power Paradox*. There were reports of sexual harassment and fraternity-style alcoholic cultures across many WeWork properties. The annual staff retreat or 'summer camp' was classic hedonism: sex, drugs, and rock 'n roll. Some of Neumann's alleged ambitions included hoping to live forever and wanting to be president of the world. He became king-like and despotic. He avoided meetings, yelled at staff, and berated them for not being better than they were.

But by 2018, WeWork had lost US$2 billion. The financial losses drew some attention, and his Tyrant shadow behaviour drove the nail in the coffin of Neumann's CEO role. The bid to launch WeWork's IPO failed. In October 2019, he stepped down from CEO and severed ties with WeWork for a payout close to US$1.7 billion.

At the end of this story, Adam Naumann still sees himself as a martyr for the cause, undermined by vindictive and jealous small thinkers. He fell from Elder to Tyrant, succumbing to the seductions of hubris and the dopamine-fuelled addictions of power.

As Elders ourselves, we can become concerned about losing power and its feel-good benefits. Our attention moves inwards. We feel afraid of looking bad, of being judged. This turns selfless behaviour to selfish, impulsive behaviour. It can become narcissism, an exaggerated admiration of one's own attributes and skills. This in turn can lead to diminished thinking.

Let's take a look at how we might avoid the shadow of the Elder, the Tyrant, and stay committed to a cause that doesn't corrupt.

BRASS TACKS

How to cultivate your Elder Archetype

Care

Expand your circle of concern. What is the biggest circle you can reach for? Start with self, friends, colleagues, business, community, nation, planet, universe, existence.

Stop labelling others. When we label others, we depict them as less than human. Notice when you sink to verbal dismissiveness.

Lead with love. Ask: "what would be an expression of love in this situation?"

Humility

Ask for help. Being humble is knowing that we cannot thrive alone. When we ask for help, we admit that we don't know everything, we can't do everything, and that we are better with others.

Ask for feedback. By asking for feedback, we invite other perspectives to help us see the parts that remain hidden to us. These are things like how we are being perceived, how we are being received, how we are affecting others, how we might improve, what we might let go of, what we can try instead. This keeps us in the mode of being a learner: a seeker of truth, beauty, and goodness.

Be grateful. Gratitude helps us to move into humility. When we are grateful, we recognise the contributions of others to our experience.

Curiosity

Practice paying attention. Curiosity allows us to see more without judgment. It keeps us asking questions, being open to new interpretations, new possibilities. When we pay attention to the world around us and the people around us, we can have a more nuanced experience. We can make new connections, new insights, new ideas.

Dig deeper with why. When we keep asking why, we explore challenges and situations from different angles. When we keep asking why, we discover new motivations, new perspectives.

Expand your experiences. Listing assumptions about a situation or a person is a great way to bring to the front what we assume is true. It can reveal default patterns, and faulty thinking.

Archetype 2: The Warrior

The Warrior seems a long way from the Elder! The name conjures battles and killing. This does not seem very compassionate. But there is something very alluring about the Warrior. We imagine fierce fighters like Xena Warrior Princess or one of these hunks from the Spartan movie *300* (2007). Aside from the potential for awesome costumes, there are aspects of the Warrior that are valuable. In more sobering circumstances, the need to fight for our right to live free becomes a real imperative not just a flight of fancy. Sometimes we need to activate the Warrior because our rights are being trampled. Let's take a look.

BOARDROOM CASE STUDY

In August 1988, the Burmese military killed thousands of people as they protested peacefully for democracy in a country now known as Myanmar. Min Thein fled the city along with others to the jungles around the border regions. There he began life as a freedom fighter, a revolutionary in a volunteer army. He led a platoon of twelve men. They had limited resources in a fight with no guarantee of success.

Corrinne Armour shared Min Thein's story with me in a podcast interview[13]. As a young adventurer, she ended up volunteering in a refugee camp where she met Min Thein. What struck Corrinne was his incredible leadership ability. How does one motivate others to put their lives on the line for a political ideal? For some it was because they had seen family murdered, and their homes set alight. It was a fight of survival. It was a fight against military dictatorship, and a fight for democracy. Every day, Min Thein reminded his platoon of what they were fighting for, connecting them to a purpose beyond their immediate needs.

Eventually, Min Thein was injured and carried by his comrades through the jungle for three days to seek medical help. He could no longer fight, so turned instead to becoming a teacher in a border camp. This is where Corrinne and he became friends, and eventually married.

In 2011, the military junta was officially dissolved following a 2010 general election, and a nominally civilian government was installed. Concerns about human rights abuses remain, even as the military maintains a huge political influence. Min Thein migrated to Australia with Corrinne. In 2019 he returned to Myanmar for the first time and has not given up his vision for a peaceful country.

---

13 Listen to the interview with Corrinne on the podcast page at www.zoerouth.com

BIG PICTURE

The Warrior Archetype

Min Thein is a modern warrior, where lives are on the line. In business, we do not often face such extreme situations. The fight to 'win' is what the Warrior Archetype offers the business leader. The Warrior Archetype has been with us since we became tribal beings. The Warrior has always played an essential role in the survival of a community: to protect the people, and to win advantages. The Warrior has taken on many forms: the Warrior Ruler and the Warrior Soldier are two examples. When we think Warrior, we often think battles, dominance and killing. This is perhaps one of the reasons the Warrior Archetype may be less favoured: violence is affiliated with the archetype. This is especially true when it comes to violence that seeks to oppress others. These are aspects of the Warrior's shadow which we shall discuss shortly. Other elements of the Warrior Archetype are worthy of inclusion.

For our context, business leadership, there are some critical elements of the Warrior we need to incorporate in our suite of roles. Courage, conviction, and determination are three of these elements.

First we need to ask, 'What is the Warrior fighting for? What are we fighting against? What are we trying to win?'

A Warrior leader fights to win. Sometimes the focus is about winning rights, like Min Thein's fight in the jungle. A Warrior might also focus on winning in business. We seek to gain a competitive edge, a larger share of the market, or triumph in difficult conditions. We see business as a game that can be won or lost. Ultimately whether winning the business game or winning rights, the outcome is about building something for the betterment of society. It's the focus on the greater good that keeps the Warrior from slipping to its shadow, the Bully. Let's look at the valuable aspects of the Warrior we can adopt.

Traits and style of the Warrior Archetype

Courage: It takes a lot of courage to stand up for what we feel is right. To call out a wrong or an injustice means holding others to account or revealing an unpleasant untruth. Our voice and perspective may not be popular or welcome. We may be ostracised and ridiculed. It is hard to take public criticism, even for what we feel is a cause larger than ourselves.

Conviction: Having conviction in our ideals and values helps us find the courage to speak up and stand out. It is only with solid reliance on our core values – ones that include and uplift humanity – that we feel able to put ourselves on the line.

Determination: Challenging hearts and minds or entrenched systems takes persistence and repeated attention. One good idea is not enough to shake others from their sleepy comfort zone. The Warrior needs to challenge repeatedly. It can be exhausting.

> When we embody the Warrior archetype, our style is persuasive and passionate. We align to a higher cause and call others to rise to the occasion. We are determined and relentless. We are fierce and focused.

Cultures created by the Warrior Archetype

Warriors tend to foster 'win first' cultures. The focus is on outcomes and achieving the objective. People are inspired by the cause and energised by the feverish intensity. The vibe is electric. This is the kind of energy that Min Thein generated to lead in his fight for democracy: this is how he led people with hardly any resources to risk their very lives for freedom.

There is a danger to these cultures in business contexts. The 'win first' culture can devolve to 'win at all costs' or 'win in spite of the costs'. Martyrdom and self-sacrifice can lead to burnout and anxiety. Win at all costs can quickly corrupt a culture hell-bent on winning. The ends justifying the means can squeeze morality aside.

It's the Warrior's shadow – the Bully – that emerges in these conditions. We'll see more of the Bully when we look at the pivot point for Warriors. For the Warrior leader, the fight is one of righteousness. The focus of winning is about elevation of all through the fight.

As Warrior leaders, we advocate:

- Justice is a just cause.
- Protecting rights is a righteous fight.
- Winning is a win for all.

Warrior leaders today

A young Warrior leader: Greta Thunberg

Born 3 January 2003, Swedish environmental activist Greta Thunberg's outspoken campaigning on climate change has gained international recognition. Thunberg organised the School Climate Strike that was replicated thousands of times around the world. In 2019, the multi-city protests involved over a million students each.

For Greta, being a Warrior leader is to fight to protect and gain rights. The fight is the right to protect the environment. The core motivation is not to triumph over others, but to triumph in favour of a principle that elevates all.

Business leaders may choose to activate the Warrior Archetype when we are faced with difficult conditions, like we are seeing in the COVID-19 pandemic, and we need to rally the troops. We are not fighting *against* an enemy but fighting for the survival of our business and community. It's this focus on what we are fighting *for*, rather than what we are fighting *against*, that helps us avoid the Warrior's shadow – the Bully.

The Warrior's shadow: The Bully

As a history buff, I'm fascinated by the rise and fall of leaders. The Netflix movie *The King* (2019) is about 'Hal', the English King Henry V, a Warrior king. He won the battle of Agincourt against bitter odds and set up the English throne for subjugation of the French. Warrior leaders like Hal are incredibly seductive. They fight for a noble cause (though subjugating the French may not be seen as 'noble' to any but the English), they reduce issues to black and white ideals, and they self-sacrifice, gallantly leading the way. That kind of energy is attractive, regardless of the morality.

This is the trap of the shadow Warrior: the Bully. We dress up reasons for battle as a 'cause'. Then we draw imaginary lines between 'us' and 'them.'

We turn to age-old stories to dress up the cause: we make it a struggle between good vs bad. The Shadow Warrior – the Bully – is divisive. They build walls, not bridges. They exclude, don't include. They see more threat and less opportunity. They see winners and losers. It's a zero-sum game.

The Bully is obsessed with results. They create 'win-at-all-cost' cultures. They play to win, and targets are everything. While these cultures can have a huge work ethic, they can turn bad quickly. Cricket Australia was known to have a 'win without considering the costs' attitude. So too did many of the banks, who fell to unethical practices just to meet targets.

Like the Warrior, the Bully is focused on *winning* – but the focus is slightly different. The Bully sees business as a competition and the objective to come out on top, to dominate or destroy the opposition. The Warrior focuses on winning, but it's winning alongside their competitor. They see their opponents as a kind of whetting stone against which they can lean and sharpen their own edge.

Bully leaders default to *exclusion*, are more suspicious, and take either an aggressive or defensive stance. Warrior leaders who default to *inclusion* want outcomes that benefit more than just their own business.

The fine line of the Warrior leader

Business leadership sometimes defines the commercial world as a battlefield. Microsoft vs. Apple, Qantas vs. Virgin. It's a good fight; may the best company win. The 'us vs. them' ethos of Warrior leaders stirs competition, compels innovation, and inoculates against complacency. There can be plenty of people stuff issues in 'win-at-all-cost' cultures: bendy ethics, silos, and aggression.

Let's compare the Warrior leader and their shadow, the Bully:

Warrior	Bully
Commitment to a cause	Commitment to winning
Values-driven	Results-driven
Win rights	Win-at-all-costs
Inclusion	Exclusion
Build bridges	Build walls

The pivot point between Warrior and Bully is **domination.**

When we feel the need to dominate anything – a game, a market, our competitors – we are allowing our shadow side to emerge. The desire to dominate comes from the ego's need to bolster oneself against others, or in spite of others. We get a false sense of superiority and satisfaction believing that if we triumph over others, that we are superior. The sense of superiority acts as a salve to a fragile ego.

How to cultivate your Warrior archetype

There are key advantages in developing a Warrior leader archetype for oneself. Fighting for a cause can galvanise action. To go above and beyond. It helps unite in search for a better future. It builds camaraderie and buy-in.

The manifesto for a Warrior leader:

- We have a commitment to a cause greater than ourselves.
- We believe that in winning rights for a cause will be of benefit to ourselves as well as to the society as a whole.
- Our values are inclusive and humanitarian.
- We seek to build bridges not walls.
- We do not see others as the enemy, but as potential allies if we can convince them of our common interests.

The Shadow Warrior – the Bully – is a seductive distraction and we need to be mindful of it, particularly if we are feeling vulnerable.

The shadow Warrior-Bully self-assessment checklist:

- Are we fighting for results to the detriment of others?
- Are we bent on 'us vs. them' where it is destruction of the other?
- Is it 'win-at-all-costs' or in spite of the costs?
- Does our gain harm others?
- Are we building walls?

If you have a purposeful cause that elevates the business and its stakeholders for the betterment of a broader audience, choose the Warrior leader archetype to guide you. Be mindful of the trigger point for the Bully: domination. It's a seductive slippery slope.

BRASS TACKS

How to cultivate your Warrior Archetype

Courage

Stand up. When we do the work of knowing deeply what our values are, and how they support the protection and development of humanity and our habitat, then we are compelled through moral duty to stand up for these values. Start by identifying what matters most, beyond our own personal and family needs. Practice perspective and zoom out to be as encompassing as we can be.

Speak up. Being a truth-teller is no easy thing. I wrote much about this in *Composure* and how when we do deep personal work to develop courage under fire, then we can feel more able to speak our truth and invite others to stand with us. It is only by sharing our voice that it might be heard.

Stand out. Being a leader means being seen and heard. We need to draw attention to our cause in visible and sometimes dramatic ways. It's not about grandstanding, but 'grace-standing'. Being a strident decrier will only alienate. When we can stand and encourage, then we can be a beacon and not a scourge. Call out wrong action, don't make people 'wrong'. People are not innately wrong, but their actions may be.

Conviction

Lead with values. Our values will range from the deeply personal to the grand universal. Lead with inclusive values and we will find our personal ones taken care of.

Uphold rights. Universal human rights are a good starting point. Where we see our rights, or those of others, being denied, we need to preserve the fundamentals of human dignity and the fragile beauty of our habitat.

Carry justice. Hold others to account for wrongs committed, if only we can help them rise to a better version of themselves. We need to carry justice for those who have lost the ability to protect themselves.

Determination

Know the path. The Warrior's path is a long one. Plan steps to bring the cause to light. Who needs to hear the message? What are their concerns? Practice zooming out in perspective to see how the cause might appeal to interests beyond the immediate, and how this might be inspiring and uplifting.

Tread the path. The Warrior needs to take action. It is not enough to be a keyboard warrior and spray venom through the internet. We need to win hearts and minds by modelling what we would have others do.

Stay the path. All Warriors can grow battle weary. It is tempting to lie down and take a break. No struggle is ever completed this way. Unerring conviction and continued action is what topples the tower.

> *"When we stand up for what we believe in – for what's right – there is always a chance that we risk the very things we fight for: our safety, our lives, our freedom. But if we stand down, the risk is definite."*
>
> – Kelseyleigh Reber

Archetype 3: The Diplomat

While the Warrior fights to win, the Diplomat talks to win. It's a less sexy approach. Gladiator garb is way more fun than a business suit! While less intense in energy, the Diplomat shines for progressing winning without destruction.

BOARDROOM CASE STUDY

John is a master of people stuff. He can read people's motivations and triggers and can adapt his style to make them feel heard. He is effusive and vivacious. He is ready with compliments and frank with honest feedback. His language can range from street talk to sweet talk.

He was facing a dilemma: two fabulous candidates vying for the Deputy CEO role.

An ambitious junior staff member, Selena, had already started manoeuvering to shore up her position as the 'obvious' replacement. This youngster was not John's preferred candidate. He had been mentoring another staff member, Georgia. She was more senior, reliable, and a quiet achiever. Georgia's style was a strong contrast to John's style, but he had faith in her competence and steadiness. The campaign was on.

John knew the only way to win over the Board and the staff was to be the consummate Diplomat. He needed to acknowledge each stakeholder's concerns and honour all the candidates while also signalling the strengths of his preferred candidate.

No one could fault John for his integrity and fairness. He treated Selena respectfully, listening to her arguments and supporting her development. He gave her fair and useful feedback. He also encouraged Georgia to be more forthright and visible in the discussions of succession. He would not fight battles for her.

In the end, the Board nominated Georgia to the role. Selena was very disappointed. John worked with her to identify strengths and skills to develop. He also worked with her on projects where she could hone these skills.

John's focus in adopting a Diplomat Archetype was to ensure a win-win-win outcome for all interested parties. Though he had his preferred candidate, he was keen to be honourable and fair to the process and the people. The 'win' he sought was for the organisation: the best person for the role to take the business forward.

BIG PICTURE

The Diplomat Archetype

The Diplomat is the epitome of skilful negotiation. Diplomats can navigate competing interests with aplomb, seeking outcomes that benefit all parties. They are trusted and venerated representatives. Sent as envoys in medieval times between courts, Diplomats were trusted to deliver messages, represent their lord/lady's interests and to negotiate on their behalf. The Diplomat often serves as the broker between factions who may not be particularly inclined to reconcile. Diplomats want a better outcome for all, and that includes the best deal for their people. There is some bend towards compromise, but there is a bottom line. Diplomat leaders see the benefit of including more perspectives. We are carefully collaborative and will look to leverage partnerships.

Diplomat leaders still have their own interests firmly planted as the key priority. We are inclusive, to a point.

The Diplomat Archetype orients towards progress and the desire to win. Like the Warrior, the focus on winning is about elevation of all. The Warrior is focused more on protecting and reclaiming rights, whereas the Diplomat seeks to win advantage. The Diplomat's core business ethos is to progress and purpose is to win. The Diplomat Archetype comes to the fore where there are competing interests, at least on the surface.

The Diplomat Archetype embodies a different relationship to power than the Warrior Archetype, or its shadow, the Bully. The Warrior uses moral force to galvanise action. The Bully uses domination to win outcomes for its own benefits. The Diplomat uses 'soft power'.

Joseph Nye introduced the concept of 'soft power' in the late 1980s. In his book *Soft Power: The means to success in world politics* (2004), he identifies that people can get others to do what they want through one or more methods: coerce them with threats, induce them with payments, or attract and co-opt them to want what you want. To achieve the latter, Nye explains that nations have three currencies that can help them exercise this soft power: culture, political values, and foreign policies crafted on moral principles. In other words, if you lead with integrity and respect in a way that others admire and aspire to, then diplomacy and soft power can ease the way for better outcomes for all.

On the other hand, hard power is the use of force to get what one wants. Hard power is a win-lose frame. Smart power is the balance between soft and hard. This is what Theodore Roosevelt referred to in his praise and adoption of the African proverb: "Speak softly and carry a big stick."

Soft power, seemingly the better option, can also be wielded for nefarious purposes. This is called 'sharp power', and it's all about manipulation. Manipulation is the shadow temptation of the Diplomat Archetype that brings on the Trickster. Before we take a look at the Trickster, let's consider the attributes of the Diplomat Archetype.

Traits and style of the Diplomat Archetype

Our demeanour is calm and detached. We maintain poise and rarely lose our cool or focus during a discussion, even if the issues are sensitive and the conversation is heated. We are socially skilled, able to heal wounded feelings, smooth over hurts, and encourage reconciliation. Diplomats ideate in good faith. We develop solutions that are of mutual benefit, not for manipulation or domination. Diplomats also negotiate in good faith. We hold stakeholders with respect and high intentions. And Diplomats work in good faith. We assume that people will honour the agreement. We expect our integrity to be the keel of the negotiation's boat.

Fairness: As Diplomats, fairness is a core principle. We want all to benefit from solutions, and we want the solutions and contributions to be equitable and satisfying.

Creativity: Diplomats know that negotiation is required because solutions are not always obvious. To find a way forward, we need to create new perspectives and opportunities for all parties. These are sometimes hidden, or not yet conceived. The ability to make new connections and ask great questions is a hallmark of successful Diplomats.

Cooperation: The spirit of the Diplomat is cooperation. The willingness to work towards a solution, together, keeps us from descending into manipulator or bully. We genuinely want to work with others to create new opportunities.

> Diplomats cultivate relationships. Slow and steadfast, relationships are built for mutual advantage, and to be called upon when needed. When we embrace the Diplomat style, we adopt a calm and centered demeanour. We are focused and detached. We are enthusiastic but not passionate. We emanate presence and reason. We are calm in chaos.

Cultures created by the Diplomat Archetype

Diplomats create calm and steady cultures. We embody respect for our opponent or fellow stakeholders and uphold principled discussions and action. When we participate in a culture led by the Diplomat ethos, we know that slow and steady wins the race. We can advocate and promote our own interests alongside those of others. We see our opponents as collaborators in mutually beneficial outcomes.

Diplomat Archetypes believe in 'persuade, don't push'. Persuasion invites buy-in. Pushing needs pressure. A sustainable agreement is one where all parties support it voluntarily rather than being coerced into it.

Soft power smooths the way. Influence with respect and invitation is better than coercion with threat and pressure. Winning in spite of the opponent is a pull towards the shadow. Winning alongside one's opponent strengthens all.

The Diplomat balances strength and softness. The principle is to treat others respectfully while also having the strength to deter and deflect any threats. The most effective Diplomats are ones who have strength to fall back on: others know that if needed, the Diplomat can activate their Warrior and move into fighting mode. When we are strong, we can be peaceful.

Diplomat leaders today

Together we are better: Angela Merkel

At the time of publication of *People Stuff*, Angela Merkel is the Chancellor of Germany, a position which she has held since 2005. She is the first female politician to do so. She has been widely described as the leader of the European Union, being its staunchest advocate. She has been crucial in developing transatlantic economic relations. She was pivotal in managing the financial crisis at the European and international level which earned her the moniker, 'the decider'. During the Syrian refugee crisis, she led the way in helping to process and support numerous refugees. In the criticism and backlash that followed, she is famous for saying "Germany suffers not from 'too much Islam' but 'too little Christianity'".[14]

She is known for being measured and even-keeled. She is methodical in her approach. She prefers cooperation to coercion. She believes in a better multilateral system and has been relentless in her pursuit of fostering global cooperation on issues like climate change.

What we can learn from Angela Merkel? Being a Diplomat is not always a popular role. We can be successful in it if we use soft power: influence and persuasion rather than force and coercion.

Diplomat demeanour is soft heart, hard hands. Compassion rules the focus, and determination rules the approach.

Values stop subterfuge. When we are clear what our values are, when we consider our collective humanity, and that all negotiations lean towards that outcome, there is no need for hiding an agenda. We only hide agendas when we are trying to leverage talks for personal gain. This is where the shadow emerges – the Trickster.

The Diplomat's shadow: The Trickster

What we sometimes call 'negotiation' is really manipulation. We get a sense of it when we observe one party's self-interest leading the conversation. My favourite legal show, *Suits*, showcases this style perfectly. Strong-arming outcomes through bribery and threats appears regularly through the episodes. Sadly, this behaviour exists in reality. This is the Trickster at work, and we can all fall into its trap.

The fine line of the Diplomat that can lead to the Trickster

In an ideal world, the Diplomat approach to negotiation is the best approach to resolving issues and bridging competing interests. We seek a win-win outcome and maintain this accord.

The reality can be somewhat different. This is where the pull to the shadow may start to occur. Influence and persuasion devolves to

---

14   Heneghan, T. (2010) Merkel urges Germans: stand up for Christian values.

use of power. Self interest and concern for our own status triggers the Trickster. Here are some signs of slipping towards the Trickster:

Pacification: This is the first sign of an imbalanced or unhealthy negotiation. Pacification is perceived as small concessions to prevent escalation of threat and violence.

Gunboat diplomacy: The name comes from the word 'gunboat', a small ship with a serious artillery power. The essence of gunboat diplomacy is flexing strength to achieve foreign policy goals.

Dollar diplomacy: This is the use of economic agreements, such as loans and licenses, to enslave a smaller nation to a bigger one.

Digital diplomacy: The use of social media and digital media to exert pressure on other governments and peoples. The scandals around the recent American elections allude to this kind of power.

People Stuff issues can arise in the Trickster's 'us first' culture:

- Duplicity
- Inauthenticity
- Passive-aggressiveness

In Trickster cultures it's all about getting ahead and putting one's own concerns above others. It's a dog-eat-dog world, where individual rights and rewards trump any collective benefits.

Let's look at the Diplomat and its shadow, the Trickster:

Diplomat	Trickster
Commitment to winning	Commitment to grandstanding
Persuasive	Manipulative
Creative	Opportunistic
Driven by win-win	Driven by win-lose
Serve	Enslave

The pivot point from Diplomat to Trickster comes when universal interest is subsumed by personal interest. The result is a default to **manipulation.**

It's such an easy thing to fall into. We are all wired for survival first. Our self-interest is always our primary concern. We have to consciously override this if our basic personal interests are threatened.

This is where the practice of perspective is critical. When we do the exercise of expanding our perspective to be as inclusive as possible, then zeroing in on the best possible choice, we see that personal interest may appear as the best solution short-term, but eventually we all pay the price for such selfishness. We saw this in the Great Toilet Paper crisis of the COVID-19 pandemic. Selfish concern for one's posterior comfort led to panic buying toilet paper supplies, leaving the poor and destitute without this basic amenity. If we could just pause a moment and consider what is in the best interest of *all*, we could avoid such dilemmas and live far more harmoniously.

BRASS TACKS

How to cultivate your Diplomat Archetype

The Diplomat Archetype is particularly useful when we are leading change that involves multiple stakeholders, often with detractors. Being able to present with steely reserve and strong compassion will help build buy-in.

When we are clear in articulating our values and remain true to them, it is difficult for others to push back against them, especially if these values are oriented towards inclusion and elevation of humanity. Pushing against that is like pushing against reeds in a river: there is no resistance and nothing to push against. Inclusive, collaborative values can help overcome our selfish, primal urges, but it takes consistent messaging and modelling to show this is a better way.

Fairness: Benefits are mutual. This is what John focused on with Selena: a fair go at the position, then a fair go at developing her skills for future roles. Successful negotiation steeped in respect means we seek outcomes that are good for all. It is much easier to dictate terms that satisfy our own requirements. If we use hard power, we can also ensure they are implemented. However, as Diplomats, soft power ensures that persuasion (not coercion) is the default approach. When we navigate conversations with the key premise of mutual benefit, we avoid the shadow pull towards manipulation.

Process is transparent. When we keep the process of discussion and decision-making clear, then we avoid backroom channels and shady dealings, where our shadow manipulator lurks.

Intention is universal. The higher good is always our north star. When we get stuck on a gritty issue, we can keep orienting towards: "what is the higher outcome we are seeking for all of us?"

Creativity: In diplomacy the best solutions are not always obvious. We need to be creative. Ask more questions. Diplomats lead best when they lead with questions. Going into a discussion with pre-conceived ideas keeps us blind to possibilities. Here we need to exercise perspective and keep seeking new creative ways of seeing. Questions help us get there.

Add more angles. Perspective helps us to see more. When we keep seeking new viewpoints, more facets and insights, more of the truth and possibilities are revealed.

Compare more ideas. Creative ideas come from connections. Seek inspiration from other industries, sectors, or countries to gain new ideas.

Cooperation: Verbal Aikido, as I described it in my book *Moments* (2016) is the practice of redirecting the argumentative energy of another person. This allows us to avoid resistance and arguments, and keep the discussion flowing to possibilities and away from obstacles.

Agree and add. We can use agreement frames. These are a neurolinguistic tool where we acknowledge someone's point of view and add to the discussion. We agree with someone's point of view and expand it: "I agree about … and this is what we also need to consider."

Challenge and add. When we feel an idea is not fully formed, or missing something, we can still encourage conversation without shutting others down. We can say: "I appreciate this part of the argument on ... and we also need to look at this part ..."

Disagree and add. Even if we disagree with someone, we can still respect their point of view. "I respect where you're coming from on ... And this is what we need to explore as well." This keeps the conversation moving.

Archetype 4: The Guardian

Both Warrior and Guardian seek to win. The Guardian however seeks to build and preserve. It's a difficult tension to manage, yet extremely useful in implementing change.

BOARDROOM CASE STUDY

Linda managed something many failed to do: lead organisational change and keep the founders happy. She was President of a volunteer association, established some 20 years ago, with long-standing traditions. The core membership, a dozen or so people, was comfortable with the status quo. Don't change what ain't broke.

Once elected to the role, Linda immediately saw the challenges ahead. Administrative processes were cumbersome. The website was outdated. The organisation membership was not appealing to a younger generation of business leaders. Dwindling membership meant the finances were going backwards. The whole thing needed a refresh.

Linda knew that radical change would only alienate the old guard. And she needed them to help support the initiatives she had in mind. She set about a campaign of 'honour and progress'. She would honour the original purpose of the organisation, publicly celebrate the achievements of the organisation, while also touting the new vision. More than that, she singled out the original members and highlighted their courage and commitment in creating an association when such a thing was an anomaly.

Over a period of two years, Linda and her team re-invigorated the organisation. The membership doubled. Events were fully subscribed and well-received. The website and marketing materials underwent a refresh. The founders were pleased to be recognised and pleased to support the new look and focus.

By honouring the past and taking the core fundamental values forward, Linda was able to hold on to the heritage of the organisation and build its future.

BIG PICTURE

The Guardian Archetype

The Guardian Archetype comes to the fore when we are focused on building an enterprise or project while still protecting people and traditions. The key mantra for the Guardian is 'don't throw the baby out with the bathwater!' As such, Guardians can feel like the handbrake to a team. They can be misunderstood and accused of being stuck in the past, often maligned for saying, "back in my day …" or "we tried that before".

The Guardian Archetype is needed when we emphasise maintaining traditions while balancing innovation and progress. The Guardian Archetype helps us to identify what matters most in our team, group, club, or business. The Guardian ensures that our values are honoured and integrated as we evolve.

In Joseph Campbell's Hero's Journey, there are two types of Guardian figures: the Herald and the Threshold Guardian. Both serve as a nudge for the hero to undertake the call to adventure.

The Herald brings news of change and seeds the call to adventure for the hero. In war movies it might be the draft notice, or announcement that war has begun. In comedies it might be the arrival of the quirky uncle coming for a family visit. The event or person signals something new is about to happen. In contemporary workplaces, the Herald might be a consultant who delivers a report on current and future trends, or even a new employee who comes with new insights and experiences.

The Herald could also be a world event like 9/11, the COVID-19 pandemic, or raging bushfires. These are signals that something is changing or needs change.

The Threshold Guardian acts as a challenger to the hero, forcing them to confront their possible future. They are there to test the hero's resolve, compel them to prove their commitment, and ensure they are ready for the next stage of their journey. In literature, Threshold Guardians might be the evil boss who denigrates the main character telling them they are good for nothing and have no future. Every underdog movie has a Threshold Guardian telling the hero they'll never amount to anything. *Rocky* (1976) is a classic film about a small-time boxer who battles low expectations to fight a champion. Sylvester Stallone's own story as the author of this script is a case in point: no one thought much of it, or of Stallone as an actor, and then he defied the odds to become a runaway success with a number of sequels. Even Albert Einstein had a Threshold Guardian. In 1895, his report form headmaster said of him, "He'll never amount to anything."

Guardians then, can be the catalyst for great achievements.

In contemporary workplaces, the Threshold Guardian might be the futurist, or the person who alerts others to the latest trends or news. They can also be seen as the doomsayer, or the devil's advocate. In our context, the Guardian serves as a challenger within the frame of preserving values and being cautious to keep what's good. It's a tricky role to play.

Traits and style of the Guardian archetype

Guardians are first and foremost, loyal. But it's not the unilateral loyalty that can get us blindsided, as I described in *Loyalty – Stop unwanted staff turnover, boost engagement, and create lifelong advocates* (2018).

Loyalty: Base your loyalty on values, not people. Charismatic leaders can charm people into being loyal. However, enduring loyalty that is based on deepest values keeps people steadfast and focused.

Caution: Caution qualifies courage. Caution helps us determine the right action for the right reasons. It doesn't dampen courage, only focuses it.

Commitment: Commitment is alignment of action to values. Commitment to act based on our values is integrity. It shows reliability and consistency that steadies others around us.

> Guardians have a strong sense of what is right and traditions we wish to uphold. We can be persuasive and passionate. Determined and focused. We blend the grace and steel of the Diplomat and the grit of the Warrior. As the Guardian can quickly be perceived as an impediment to change and progress, instead of advocating this, we seek to anticipate the need for balance in our argument. As Guardians we always advocate change that embraces the best of tradition, building upon it, instead of sweeping it aside.

Cultures created by the Guardian archetype

Guardians foster deeply loyal and passionate cultures. We rally people around core values and current practices for the contribution they have made over time. Guardians are community-oriented and welcoming. We focus on a sense of belonging to the group and to a vision steeped in powerful symbols.

Choose carefully. It's not change for change's sake, it's change for the right sake. Change begins with celebrating what's working and valuable. We need to evaluate options against trends and consequences.

Act wisely. We need to preserve what matters most. Protect core values. Promote change that builds towards our vision.

Respond consistently. Steadfast is steady. We need to be consistent with our filter of values. We need to always come back to core principles: is this making things better for more people, place, and planet?

Honour the past, forge the future: Peter FitzSimons

Peter FitzSimons is an Australian author, journalist, radio and television presenter, and a former rugby union player for the Wallabies. He has also been Chair of the Australian Republican movement since 2015.

Like many Australian Republicans, FitzSimons believes it's time for Australia to nominate its own head of state. As a constitutional monarchy, the English monarch is currently the official head of state, with a Governor General nominated by the Prime Minister as the Queen's representative in the country. The Governor General's role is largely ceremonial, and the Queen has never denied a nomination.

Why become a Republic? FitzSimons says[15] that it's time for us to grow up as a nation and be fully independent. The constitutional monarchy reminds us of a colonial past that brought much suffering for Australian Aboriginal people. He says: ""Let's not forget that this

---

15   Wingerei, K. (7 October 2018). Peter FitzSimons and Australia's search for independence.

country has been populated not just since 1788, but for over 60,000 years."

FitzSimons is an interesting example of a Guardian navigating the tension between preserving traditions while building a new future. What do we need to preserve as a people as we build a unique Australian identity moving forward? How do we choose what to bring along and which bits to let go? Some in the Republican movement suggest:

- Bring with us our long and complex Aboriginal history and traditions, language, and knowledge and connection with the land.
- The Aussie spirit of mateship and having a fair go.
- Our burgeoning multi-cultural society with all its vivid colours and flavours of the world.
- Our love of sport and the great outdoors.

What we want to leave behind:

- Connection to our colonial past and a nostalgic attachment to a monarch from a different hemisphere and continent.

Only by letting go of some parts can we build a new Australia, fully autonomous, and capable of forging its own path and identity, unique and distinct from what has gone before.

FitzSimons does a good job of honouring all the threads of history and weaving a new tapestry. This is a great example of broad perspective, expanding the vision to be as inclusive as possible, and then zooming in to focus on what is most important. By honouring the best bits of the combined history, while acknowledging the travesties of the past, his arguments show both compassion and wisdom.

One of the challenges we face when we embody the Guardian archetype, is slipping into its shadow – the Fanatic. We become so attached to our cause, so caught up in the conviction we are right, we become blinkered.

The Guardian's shadow archetype: The Fanatic

We are wired to fear change because of unknown threats. Through the ages, we build walls to keep others, the unknown, out. From castles to fences, from the Berlin Wall to the great Wall of China.

The leaders who advocate for walls are Fanatic leaders, disguised as Guardians. Our conviction in what is right can obscure our perspective and bring the blinkers up. We can get tunnel vision when we allow our beliefs to elevate as truth, the only truth. If we allow our conviction to take over, we may become obsessed with building an empire based on our version of the truth, on our terms.

As Fanatics we want to keep business and people safe by controlling the variables. As such we can end up advocating for an 'us only' culture. Others can get lost. Though keen to build the business, as Fanatics we can be reluctant to test radical ideas, and prefer a safe, stable and homogenous workplace. We want to maintain a steady, status quo march forward. While stability and loyalty can be valuable, we can fall victim to disruption, lagging behind competition.

There are plenty of people stuff issues in 'us only' Fanatic-led cultures:

- Change resistance
- Negativity
- Poor buy-in

Any change becomes a threat to the norm, and status quo becomes the default argument. Fear reigns instead of sensible caution. Exclusion is the sign we have tipped from Guardian to Fanatic. The trigger to this tipping point is **blind conviction.**

Let's compare what happens between Guardian and Fanatic:

Guardians	Fanatics
Include	Exclude
Commitment to growth	Commitment to domination
Loyal	Selfish
Build others	Build self
Driven by caring	Driven by fear
Protect	Destroy

Boris Johnson, Prime Minister of the United Kingdom shines as a Fanatic masquerading as a Guardian. He claimed the Prime Minister role through his bid to lead Brexit, Britain's departure from the European Union. Spouting the desire to protect Britain's interests (a strong Guardian principle), Johnson is strongly nationalistic and heralds tradition and protecting the British identity. However, the blinkers on perspective come up and he moves to be exclusive rather than inclusive in his point of view – tipping towards being a Fanatic. His strong populist rhetoric appeals to those who would keep Britain 'British' (in other words, white and English-speaking).

We know we are following in the Fanatic footsteps if we maintain an 'exclude' clause in our point of view. Everyone except for those groups are part of our group. If we find ourselves falling into this pattern of thought, we know we have let our values slip a rung and our perspective narrow. We set ourselves up for confrontations and prejudice instead of building something fantastic based on inclusive values. This is what FitzSimons manages to avoid in his advocacy for a Republic: it's not Australia against the British, it's all of us, together, on a new path of our own making.

BRASS TACKS

How to cultivate your Guardian Archetype

The practice of perspective helps shape our Guardian Archetype. Let's see this in action.

Loyalty

Clarify loyalty to values. What are the values that govern all our choices? How inclusive are they? This is about exercising the expand aspect of perspective.

Clarify loyalty to beliefs. What are the beliefs that articulate our values? Are they wise and compassionate? This is balancing sensible and sensitive choices.

Clarify loyalty to a cause. What is the cause we are advocating? Does it support a better future for all? By exercising perspective we can choose a cause that benefits more of us.

Caution

Assess risk. What might we lose if we proceed? Is this in line with our values? How much is fear filtering our perspective? This is being discerning.

Monitor trends. What is the bigger picture? How are trends affecting our view of the world and what we feel is most important? How will these trends shift our values and beliefs? How will these trends affect our ability to make decisions based on our values and beliefs? This is distilling choices to the best ones.

Evaluate benefits. What opportunities does a new direction bring for us? Will this add benefits for more people? Will our gain create gain for others? Again, we are distilling and discerning with wise and compassionate filters.

Commitment

These steps are wisdom in action:

Disagree in discussion. Robust challenges help clarify our thinking.

Bring us back to what matters most: values and beliefs, inclusion and benefits for all.

Agree in decisions. Once the decision is made in alignment to values and vision, support it and show a united front.

Follow through on resolutions. Be consistent by following through on the resolutions made.

The Guardian exemplifies sensible caution. The Pioneer readies us for courageous action.

Archetype 5: The Pioneer

Like the Guardian, the Pioneer seeks to build business. The key difference is the approach towards risk and experimentation. The Guardian seeks to preserve what was good from traditions while cautiously edging forward. The Pioneer seeks to craft something new altogether.

BOARDROOM CASE STUDY

Ilea Buffier is a woman on a mission. Her intent? Zero carbon organisations. Her method? Implement carbon tracking software called Evalu8 Sustainability. Once installed in a business, it assesses the business' spending, and makes suggestions for changes that will save it money and reduce or eliminate carbon emissions. This allows the business owner to save money and be carbon neutral. Ethical and profitable. Good business and good planetary citizen all in one. It's brilliant!

This project gnawed at Ilea for over 17 years. Like any calling, she just couldn't put it down, in spite of the many setbacks from contracts, contractors, designers, and more. She worked relentlessly to gather the team and resources to bring it to fruition.

To listen to Ilea is to see the future we long for made real, now. Her approach is pragmatic, not evangelical. She draws people to her cause because it does not cost more to do the right thing, but doing the right thing saves on costs. She knows she is guiding people's ethical decisions by lining their pockets through more beneficial decisions. But a Pioneer knows this too: if it is to work, it will need to appeal to more than aspirations and virtue, it needs to strengthen the bottom-line. Good for the individual, good for the business, good for the planet. Smart pioneers know it's easy to be virtuous when it serves our own personal needs and desires.

BIG PICTURE

The Pioneer Archetype

The challenge for the Pioneer is dealing with the unknown. To pioneer means to chart new territory, to venture out, to seek a new way of living and being in the world. Uncertainty can act as a giant tether to the status quo. Because the future is uncertain and unknown, and the method untried, there are a lot of risks associated with taking on a pioneer project.

The Pioneer is best called upon when we want to build and progress. Growth and development is our imperative. Experimentation and pathfinding is our method. The spirit of adventure drives the Pioneer.

In North American and Australian cultures, the Pioneer Archetype is particularly active. In North America, Europeans left for the 'new world' in droves, seeking a better life where they could forge their own way. Settlers ventured across the seas and unfamiliar lands to trial a new way of living and working in new communities. In Australia, the migrant story followed the convict one: many in England were exiled to Australia or sentenced to work camps to build roads and bridges. Once their term was completed, the convicts were allowed into the fledgling Australian communities to forge a new life for themselves.

The pioneering stories in both these continents exist alongside the tales of genocide and conflict with the Indigenous people who were already living on these 'new' lands. This is the part of the Pioneer Archetype we must heal and reclaim. Any new Pioneer story needs to be tempered with the wisdom and compassion of the Elder: a better world for all, not just for some.

Traits and style of the Pioneer Archetype

Adventure: Adventure begets experience, and from experience we can derive good judgment. When we try something new and exciting, we create new experiences from which we can draw observations and insights, adding to our wisdom bucket.

Experimentation: An insatiable curiosity helps to test a stubborn reality. If we are stuck in a rut, we can run experiments to try new approaches. From thought through to action, we can explore different ways of being, thinking and doing.

Optimism: Look forward. There are no eyes in the back of our head. A forward focus keeps the momentum forward too. When we look where we might go, we have a better chance of getting there.

> The Pioneer has a unique focus. The Warrior aligns strongly to a cause, the Diplomat focuses on sound win-win outcomes and respectful processes, and the Guardian obsesses with preserving what's best about culture and tradition.
>
> For the Pioneer, there is a survival tinge to our future focus. There is a creeping element of 'will this work?' in all of our activity. The Pioneer is rigorous and relentless. We inspire others with possibilities, and model commitment to see the end game through. We love being on the edge of discovery. First at the prow of the ship, searching the horizon. Our enthusiasm is infectious.

Cultures created by the Pioneer Archetype

Pioneers inspire. Pioneers see possibilities and communicate with enthusiasm. Pioneers galvanise others in pursuit of a better future, a leader's greatest gift and core responsibility. Cultures led by the Pioneer are vibrant and dynamic. These cultures are characterised by robust discussions, respectful challenging of ideas, constructive disagreement, and enthusiastic championing of novel and unique ideas. They are versatile and adaptable.

The people stuff problems that can arise in a Pioneer-led culture include overwork and burnout. A commitment to experimentation and testing can lead to pressing deadlines that amp up stress and drive mono-focus on outcomes, forgetting process.

Atlassian, a Pioneer culture, has found a way around this by having team coaches. The team coaches help the team to look at their process, not just the results. The coach inserts a break or pause into the workflow so that the players (as they call them) have a chance to catch their breath and take perspective on process.[16] It's a great way of protecting against the pitfalls of the Pioneer.

The Pioneer has three core principles: Test ideas. Take risks. Try again.

Test ideas.

How good is the idea? Only by testing it will we discover if it's worth fighting for. Like throwing a bone to a dog: if it's a good one, they'll hang on. Juicy ideas create raving fans.

Take risks.

Life has a way of triumphing in the most unlikely of places. A tree clinging to a rock face only lives because a seed risked everything to sprout in tenuous ground. Growth needs movement, and that often means taking a risk – to risk new territories, new actions, new projects. Anything new is a risk. Anything the same is also a risk. We risk much when we risk nothing. One can lead to breakthroughs, the other to breakdowns. Choose new. It gives us more choices.

---

16 Listen to my interview with Bernie Ferguson from Atlassian on the podcast page at zoerouth.com

Try again.

Defeat is temporary. Defeat and failure are simply a course correction. We need to take the lessons in defeat and apply them to the next experiment.

Pioneer leaders today

> *"If you get up in the morning and think the future is going to be better, it is a bright day."*
> – Elon Musk

One of the most noteworthy Pioneers is Elon Musk. Educated as an engineer, Musk became a dynamic technology entrepreneur. As the co-founder of PayPal, he took the millions he made from the sale of this venture to establish a number of radically progressive organisations. It's hard to know which business to mention first – they are all impressive in their own right. He is the co-founder, CEO and product architect of Tesla, an electronic car manufacturing company. This was established with the overarching objective of ending fossil fuel dependence. He is the founder, CEO, and chief engineer/designer of SpaceX, an aerospace manufacturer and space transportation services company. Added to this already amazing list of companies, he formed the Boring Company, an infrastructure and tunnel construction company, with the objective of solving traffic congestion issues.

While these are his immediate commercial interests, Musk's famous intention is to colonise Mars and help make the human race an inter-planetary civilisation. He is deeply concerned about the future of humanity and is seeking its perpetuation on other planets.

In case that wasn't enough, he is the co-founder of Neuralink, a medical technology company working on a computer-brain interface. Its first application is to assist brain injury patients with becoming mobile by bypassing their impaired spinal cord messages via the computer interface to control their limbs once more.

While Musk's initiatives have made him personally wealthy, money is not now the primary objective. He has dedicated all his endeavours to the improvement of the human race.

There are costs to such wild and unstoppable pioneering energy. Multiple sources cite Musk's demanding and exacting approach as a leader. He works countless hours, sacrificing sleep and health. The pace and intensity of all his projects are breathtaking, and his teams scramble to keep up. They are borne aloft by his vision for the future. It's worth asking if his Pioneer vision is worth the shadows of the other archetypes that creep in: the Bully, the Tyrant, and the Fanatic. Let's hope he survives his own pace and shadows to see his visions fulfilled.

Like other archetypes, the Pioneer has a shadow. The thrill of adventure and gain can unleash the Gambler.

The Guardian's shadow: The Gambler

Henry was a successful businessman. He co-founded a popular recruitment agency and was quickly known as a young gun with a magic touch. He expanded the service to two more cities, leveraging his client goodwill and burgeoning reputation. He sunk a lot of capital into the new premises and took on more debt to boost the profile of the business in the new cities.

Entrepreneurs sought him out. They wanted his advice and mentoring on how to scale fast. His pride swelled as he dispensed wisdom from his five-year rocket ride in business. After relocating from a regional town to a major metropolitan hot spot, Henry savoured the fast pace of city nightlife. A friend invited him to nightclubs and he started to party hard.

Henry spent more and more time at casinos and speakeasies. At first, it was to soak up the party atmosphere. He started experimenting with some of the illicit substances traded under tables in a bid to build rapport with some big wig financiers who were seeking other lucrative ventures.

In the meantime, texts and calls from his team were ramping up. They were drowning in the pressure to get a foothold in the bigger, more competitive markets. The books were red and haemorrhaging each month. They'd lost a few star performers over concern for the state of the business.

By that stage, Henry was using harder drugs. What had started as an experiment was now a crutch to help him focus after the late nights. He was juggling the different businesses and their attention. His wife Janine had had enough. She packed up one of their cars and returned to their home base in regional Victoria.

Alone now, with creditors calling, Henry broke down. No one saw him for six weeks. In his absence, the company went into receivership. A skeleton crew was hanging on by a thread in the original office, looking to secure new jobs before they too bailed for safer ports.

A friend drove Henry to a rehab centre. He was there for six months. Things were never the same again.

The fine line of the Pioneer leader

What turns a pragmatic pioneer into a reckless gambler?

Research suggests[17] it's the attractiveness of uncertain rewards. Playing a game where the outcome is known is no fun at all. It's the tension of not knowing how it will turn out that drives excitement in the game. This is why the uncertainty of the game drives illogical, maladaptive behaviour. Pioneers who get a taste for the game of creating and testing can fall into this trap too.

Let's look at what happens at the cusp between Pioneer and Gambler:

Pioneer	Gambler
Calibrated optimism	Untethered craving
Planned adventure	Careless misadventure
Test and review	Bet and bat
Take measured risks	Take unqualified risks
Opportunity to grow	Opportunity to win

---

17   Anselme, P. and Robinson, M. (Dec 2, 2013). What motivates gambling behaviour? Insight into dopamine's role.

The turning point for a Pioneer to Gambler is **the selfish pursuit of uncertain rewards.** We get distracted by the thrill and forget to evaluate the consequences, for ourselves and for others. Whenever we narrow our perspective without being discerning, we become blinkered.

Risk can be mitigated considerably by perspective. When we zoom out and observe the patterns of our emotions and the patterns of our behaviour, we can see the causation-consequence link. We can see the biochemical response to established environmental triggers that have us anticipating the thrill of an uncertain game. In recognising this we can be mindful of containing it. Just like a horse's ears prick up and its steps become more energetic, our inner drivers pick up and we can feel the surge of excitement within us. To rein the horse in, we talk to it in a reassuring way and apply pressure on the reins to interrupt its forward motion. We can do that for ourselves too: talk ourselves down from the hype and apply pressure by changing activity. We can do this with a walk, or changing focus, or being present with loved ones. It gently brings us back to other forms of renewal and energy – ones that are pro-social rather than destructive.

BRASS TACKS

How to cultivate your Pioneer Archetype

Adventure

Explore horizons. Horizons have a way of calming the spirit and opening the mind. Horizons reveal possibilities in their expanse.

Seek the novel. There is comfort in the familiar. There is opportunity in the new. When we experience new things we can make new connections, new observations, and new mental models.

See with new eyes. The ordinary can be extraordinary when we choose to see through a different lens: see with eyes of a child, a chicken, an ant, a giant. See how things we look at shift in meaning and appearance.

Experimentation

Try new things. When was the last time you tried a new skill? To be a beginner again at something demands humility and openness. One cannot jump from novice to expert without fumbling and finding a way through. In this way we can discover ability and opportunities. Maybe even community too!

Combine different things. New ideas often come from connections between unrelated subjects, creating new magical possibilities. What crazy things could we combine to create a new future?

Get feedback. Don't just ride a hunch! Any scientist knows that all experiments create results to test a hypothesis. Getting feedback from the experiment from different sources helps to understand the opportunity, or lack of it, in the process we've trialled.

Optimism

Cultivate belief. To go where no one has gone before requires belief in possibility, not certainty. Cultivate that.

Anticipate success. Be prepared for failed experiments. Be also prepared for the possibility of a successful one. When we know the destination, we can keep seeking a route through the wilderness.

Track progress. There is nothing more demotivating than a lot of effort with no progress. The destination is one milestone, mark others along the way. One small increment of success can boost morale and create traction for ongoing effort.

Now that we have explored perspectives on self through the archetypes, we can turn our gaze to one of the more challenging aspects of people stuff: other people.

PART FOUR

THEM

Perspective on others

So far, we've explored the practice of perspective as a meta skill, and then how we might see ourselves and our role relative to business purpose. We've looked at various archetypes to help us channel the best leadership approach. Along the way, we've exposed some of the challenges that we face as leaders when it comes to our own failings: the shadow archetypes. With each shadow, there is a trigger that tips us from the positive intentions of the main archetype to its shadow. For the Elder, the trigger is hubris and arrogance. For the Warrior, it's power and domination. For the Diplomat, it's status and manipulation. For the Guardian, it's conviction and needing to be right. For the Pioneer, it's the thrill of winning an uncertain game. All of these shadow triggers occur with one major shift: a shift from focus on others to a focus on self. When our perspective turns inwards and becomes self-concerned, we become blind and blinkered, and our shadow emerges.

If these patterns exist in us, they exist in others too. The archetypes and shadows are one map for understanding human dynamics. In this next section, we explore an additional map that is founded on neuroscience. We will take a look at basic biochemistry and neurotransmitters. As we do, we reveal that it is fear of loss that triggers our dark side, what I call the Four Devils.

In this chapter we look at some of the most difficult people stuff behaviours we need to contend with, and how we can respond and manage these challenges. On the surface, these people stuff challenges look awful. The practice of perspective helps us zoom out and see the patterns and triggers, so that we can take wise and compassionate action. We demystify people stuff and create simple steps to start wading through the muck. Based on many challenging situations I've helped leaders with, we will use the following composite fictional case study to unpack the Four Devils and some solutions for dealing with them.

BOARDROOM CASE STUDY

The characters

Peter: CEO of a mid-sized retail company with a warehouse and online shopping. The executive team had been going from strength to strength under his command.

Stanley: Head of Corporate Services. Seasoned leader, well-established career.

Gemma: Head of Client Service. Recent arrival with a broad range of experience in multiple industries.

David: Chief Information Officer. Quiet achiever.

Stephanie: Head of Marketing. Began her career with the company, experience across divisions.

Scene 1

At first, Stanley liked Gemma, the newest team member and head of client service. She was fun and friendly. She was courteous and respectful. She asked good questions and loved a laugh.

Then she started to make suggestions. Some were really great – like adding an AI response service on the website to answer basic questions for customers, 24/7. She also proposed ideas for building executive group rapport, like team beach retreats and Formula 1 corporate box seats. Pricey suggestions, but fun.

Then Gemma started recommending how to organise the warehouse better. She volunteered to work with the team to set it up.

Stanley bristled at this. The warehouse fell under corporate services, his area and his remit. He knew an adversary when he saw one. Gemma was new to the business, with fresh ideas and plenty of energy. She had a lot to say. On everything – including Stanley's area of corporate services. No way was he going to let an upstart muscle in on his territory. Gemma needed to know her place.

Scene 2

Every chance he got, Stanley called out Gemma's overstepping. He mentioned it in meetings. He went to Peter the CEO and complained, politely, about the infringements. Stanley campaigned against her ideas in corridor conversations with colleagues, mentioning Gemma's growing megalomania and interference. Pretty soon the staff meetings prickled with tension.

Gemma found herself isolated and frustrated that her good ideas couldn't get any traction. She saw the way forward clearly, as she had plenty of experience in those business development areas. Her enthusiasm started to wane, and her discontent rose. Gemma found herself crying in the parking lot on Monday mornings. She dragged her sulkiness with her throughout the day. She tended to weep in the staff kitchen while making tea. Her colleagues would do an about-face if they saw her in there.

Scene 3

Gemma's feelings of isolation and under-appreciation spilled over to team meetings where she found herself shaking with rage as agenda points were pushed through without considering her contributions. She left many meetings in tears. The others grew tired of consoling her in the bathroom and left her to sob it out.

David, the Chief Information Officer, did not like what he was seeing. He saw how Stanley was treating Gemma and took her side. David preferred to keep his two cents to himself, just getting on with his work. But the antagonism between Gemma and Stanley bothered him.

He too grew emotive. He started to get angry about the issues. He blamed Peter the CEO and started to criticise him. David became more and more vocal and aggressive. Others objected to David's attitude and moved to shut him down in meetings.

Scene 4

Stephanie, the longest serving team member and head of marketing, had seen it all before. She knew the cancer had to be cut out, and fast. She was worried about the effect on the team's outputs. They were on target to hit their best results yet, and she knew this kind of bickering would lead to productivity declines. She also knew that if one of them left she would be the one who would have to pick up the pieces, since she knew the most about the organisation. She was busy enough already! She didn't have the time or inclination to sort them out. That was the CEO's job anyway. Plus, she hated conflict.

She initiated closed door meetings with Peter about the culture. She reported Stanley's undermining. She told the CEO how Gemma's moods were causing others to walk on eggshells. She pointed out David's aggression as unprofessional. Something needed to be done about this. It was compromising people's sense of safety at work.

Outside the CEO's office, Stephanie was nice as pie. She made small talk with everyone, maintaining good relationships with each of them. She assured each person she knew where they were coming from and that she empathised.

Scene 5

The CEO was exasperated. Why couldn't they just get along and do their job? He was sick of fielding Stanley's complaints about Gemma. Gemma was an emotional wreck who dropped into tears every time he looked at her. David was getting harder and harder to deal with, defaulting to arguments on any topic. Thank goodness for Stephanie. She seemed to be getting along OK with everyone.

He was at a loss. The team had started so well! They were making progress and had been enjoying each other's company. Sales were up and plans to launch their best selling products in new markets were underway. How did it turn bad so quickly?

Peter stewed on it. He reviewed everything he did with the team. Had he been too lenient? Was he being too trusting? Did he need to play the heavy in this conflict? Was he playing favourites? He felt the full weight of loneliness and isolation in the top job.

Peter's doubt in his own leadership grew like fungus on his thoughts. He became broody and snapped at people. He was finding himself more and more behind a closed door. He just needed a break.

Observations

It's easy to put labels on the people with these behaviours. We might call Stanley an asshole, Gemma a princess, David a bully, and Stephanie a two-faced piece of work. And the CEO? Lame. But this is not what people-savvy people do. We don't label people, we label behaviours. We don't make people wrong, we deal with wrong behaviours. While we need to address behaviour that is problematic, we also need to deal with the underlying patterns creating that behaviour.

Let's take a deeper dive.

The turbulent Four Devils

If you've worked in a team before, likely you've experienced some form of turbulence. There can be good days, then days when things get rough, just like the weather.

Consider the four elements of wind, water, fire, and earth. The interactions can either be pleasant or unpleasant. A gentle combination of wind and water can be a lovely experience on a hot summer's day. Imagine sitting on the beach, sun beaming, and a lovely breeze stirring gentle waves. If the wind picks up, the sky darkens, and the waves become rough and treacherous.

People are elemental too. When we feel calm, things go well. When we are agitated, storms brew and unleash havoc. We experience the agitation of others through these four primal forces:

1. Communication
2. Behaviour
3. Emotions
4. Beliefs

Emotions and beliefs belong to our internal world. Behaviour and communication are the outer expression of this internal world.

I have mapped these against the four natural elements: wind, water, fire, and earth. In the model below we get our first glimpse of what drives the Four Devils, which we will go into greater depth later on.

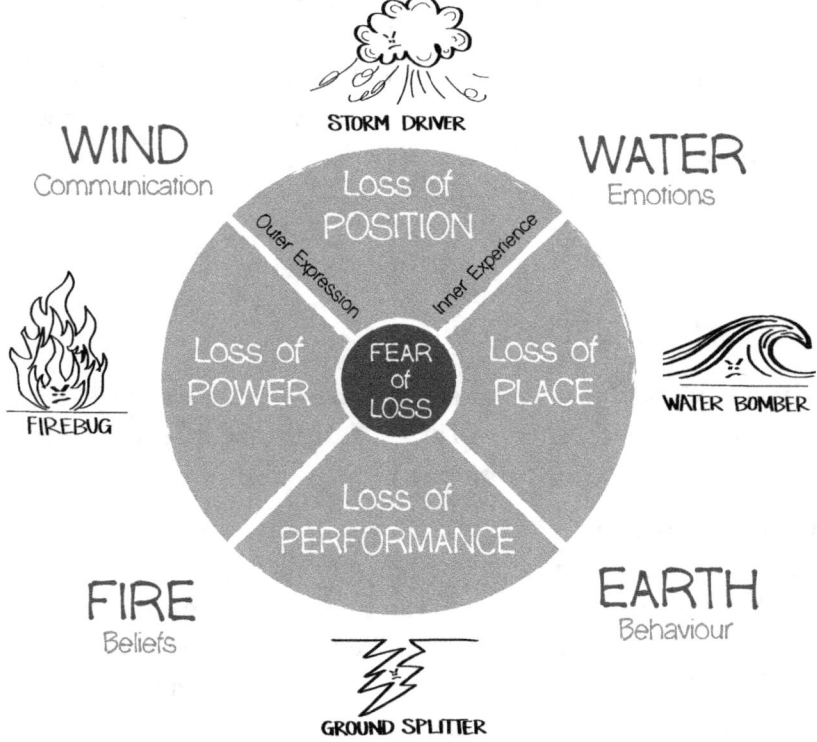

Figure 7: The Four Devils

Let's work our way through the elements.

The horizontal axis is our INNER EXPERIENCE.

It consists of:

- Beliefs – the fire element
- Emotions – the water element.

Beliefs drive emotions and emotions reinforce beliefs. This can be a positive or negative reinforcing loop.

The vertical axis is our OUTER EXPERIENCE.

It has:

- Communication – verbal expression of our thoughts and feelings – the wind element.
- Behaviour – physical expression of our thoughts and feelings – the earth element.

At the centre is the primary driver of the Four Devil chaos: fear of loss. To understand this primary driver, we need to understand the primal elements that create it. These are our biochemicals.

People are complex biochemical creatures. Throw us together in an organisation and we get all sorts of chemical reactions, good and bad. When we know something is happening biochemically, we can take actions to set up teams and individuals for positive experiences and avoid negative ones. This is how we can keep the Four Devils from emerging.

Our biochemistry has primitive origins, designed for survival. It's a heady cocktail mix designed to ensure we endure as a species. Let's take a look at our biochemical survival soup.

Ingredient #1: Dopamine

Dopamine feels good. It's a little inner rush when we accomplish something. When we had to hunt for survival, we got a shot of this chemical when we spotted prey. Hunting is hard work, and our bodies helped us keep doing it with a little neurochemical supercharger. The anticipation of the chase and kill felt really good, thanks to dopamine. Nowadays this is the feel-good boost we get when we find something we lost, or when we come across something unique and interesting, or when we complete a task. It's one of the reasons why email is so addictive: every time we delete it, or process it, we get a shot of dopamine. That little surge of interest when we see social media notifications? Dopamine. New unread emails piquing curiosity? Dopamine. Crossing out something on our to-do list? Dopamine. Essentially, work structures set us up to seek out dopamine all day long. This is good and bad news for productivity. We gravitate towards the tasks that give us quick rewards. This can lead us to avoid the more difficult tasks as they have less dopamine benefits.

Ingredient #2: Oxytocin

This is the trust drug. It surges when we have pleasant physical contact with others like a handshake, a pat on the back, or a hug. It gets released when we have strong, positive social interactions with others. Well-bonded teams have goops of oxytocin swishing between them. When we frequented caves, the need for oxytocin and fitting into the group helped us to follow group rules and norms. Oxytocin helps us cooperate and activate pro-social behaviour.

Ingredient #3: Serotonin

This is a strong social biochemical that is the feel-good sensation of pride and well-being. We get it through improvements of social standing and status. Wanting to stand out in a crowd when we roamed the plains helped us to attract mates and reproduce, ensuring the survival of our species. Wanting to be better, and to be seen as better, triggered improvement behaviours. Feel good about a promotion? Serotonin. Got recognised as a standout employee? Serotonin. Got some applause for your presentation? Yup, serotonin. Even seeing others get recognised can cause a serotonin surge.

Ingredient #4: Endorphins

Often associated with exercise, this happiness drug also gets released when we laugh, and when we cry. It helps us release and process emotions, triggering empathy and intimacy. We can also get a boost of endorphins when we rush to meet a deadline and work under pressure.

Ingredient #5: Cortisol

Cortisol is our internal alarm system. It triggers survival behaviour when we are threatened. If it's an acute threat, then cortisol surges and we experience that as fear. If it's more of a general concern, cortisol seeps slowly, and we experience that as anxiety. Disappointment, loss, and fear of loss trigger boatloads of cortisol. When this happens, our vision narrows and our executive brain function is stood aside temporarily. Our heart rate goes up, our breathing goes shallow, and we are primed to fight, freeze, or flee. When we are in this state, the only perspective we have is to protect against loss. When this happens, our shadow takes over.

This is how the Four Devils are unleashed. Fear of loss dumps cortisol in our system and we become focused on survival. When we were tribal beasts, this was a primitive hide or fight reaction. Nowadays, the same impulses exist. They present as unhelpful, sometimes antisocial, and definitely unproductive team behaviours.

As leaders, we need to learn how to decode these signals and then ease the triggers.

BIG PICTURE

Fear of loss

Here's the thing about biochemicals: they feel awesome. But when we experience a threat to what creates the feel-good ones, we get agitated. We get charged with cortisol and go into an unhelpful state. We can get angry, frustrated, and experience tunnel vision. This is the fight-or-flight response.

Fear of loss is the biggest driver of unproductive and unfriendly interactions.

Fear of loss drives turmoil through people stuff dimensions.

These fears were identified in David Rock's neuroscience research in *Your Brain At Work: Strategies for overcoming distraction, regaining focus, and working smarter all day long.* (2009). He discovered the common contemporary workplace triggers that cause a primal defensive reaction into survival mode. He called this an 'amygdala hijack'. Our amygdala is responsible for our flight-or-fight response. When triggered, we lose full access to our executive brain functions, and are primed instead for survival: fight, flight, or freeze. In this state, we lose our ability to think things through rationally, our blood pressure is elevated, our heart rate increases, our breathing may become shallow, our vision becomes focused, and our short-term memory is disturbed. We may become irritable, jumpy, or distracted. With more acute responses, we may become argumentative, belligerent, angry, frustrated, teary, or shut down.

The most difficult of human behaviour often comes from someone experiencing an amygdala hijack, either an acute response, or one that is sustained over time from chronic stress.

David Rock created the acronym of SCARF to capture these amygdala provoking triggers: loss of status, certainty, autonomy, relatedness, and fairness. Overwork is another trigger, but it doesn't fit nicely in the acronym! I've overlayed his findings against the common patterns in behaviour, emotions, communication, and beliefs. When the triggers combine, they can turn us into devils: amygdala-primed survival demons! We're hard to deal with, and hard to lead. To tackle this unrest in our lives, we must first examine our fears.

We may fear loss of power, loss of position relative to others, loss of place relative to the group, or loss of performance. All of these are linked to our biochemical soup. We fear losing the feel-good biochemicals and the conditions that generate them. Power is linked to status and serotonin. Position is also linked to status and serotonin. Place within the group is linked to oxytocin. Performance is linked to dopamine. Losing any of these conditions triggers cortisol and our survival reactions.

The fear of loss – loss of power, position, place, and performance – lies at the very centre of people stuff problems. Once we've dealt with the causes of this fear, then we can look at how to deal with the outcomes.

Fear of loss is the key to understanding the unruliness in people stuff. Let's explore it further.

1. Loss of power

As we discovered in the chapter about Elders, power is not something that is taken, but something that is granted. When power and status is granted to us and we get dopamine (from the sense of accomplishment) and serotonin (from the new status and recognition) we can become bedevilled by the feel-good sensations it brings. We seek it out and want to control others as a result. Power is an energy that we have long danced with. It is seductive. Power gives an illusion of safety. We think that by controlling others, by exerting authority, that we will be protected from harm, and we will maintain the serotonin and dopamine.

The other challenge is when power over our own choices appears to be taken from us, it pushes us into survival mode. When change is imposed on us (like going through a restructure, being forced into self-isolation, or being made redundant), we can lash out in unhelpful ways by being defensive or aggressive.

In our company Boardroom case study, Stanley sees Gemma's suggestions as threats to his power and reacts defensively.

The only thing we truly have power over is ourselves. We have power over our thoughts, our emotions and our choices. Most of us are not taught to harness this inner energy, so we fall victim to thinking we can find security outside of ourselves.

> *"The day the power of love overrules the love of power, the world will know peace."*
> – Mahatma Gandhi

2. Loss of position

Status feeds self-worth. We seek safety by knowing our place within the tribe, team or organisation. Status often comes with privileges that we imagine we have earned through commitment to an organisation or through outstanding performance. We feel a sense of worth through our status achievements. We feel a stronger sense of self when we achieve ranks in made-up games like promotions. The serotonin rush keeps us seeking more and fearing its loss.

Gemma is motivated to shore up her status. It blinds her to the repercussion of her behaviour.

Status determines who gets what. From primitive tribes through to modern organisations, we use status to determine who gets what portion of the bounty. It applies to things like office size, desk location, job titles, and parking spaces. Fairness is determined by made up status rules.

This is what picks at David: he does not like the unfair treatment of Gemma.

Of all the triggers to fear, loss of position comes closest to a real survival threat. Status changes can mean that some miss out while others benefit. When we have our sense of self keenly tied to status, this hurts a lot.

It's also a false paradigm.

Our real worth is not in the status we gain, or in the spoils we accumulate. Our real sense of worth is in how we think of ourselves. How our actions align with our values. Our kindness. Our diligence. The other false paradigm is that 'more is better'. In fact, we need a lot less than we imagine to lead a comfortable and happy life. A better question to explore is 'how much is enough?' When we know how much is enough, we get less anxious and aggressive about getting our 'fair' share, since we already have plenty. The 'how much is enough' question becomes, "how do we make sure there is enough for everyone?"

In the meantime, fear of losing status and its serotonin payoff can trigger our fight and flight response, and cue the devils.

3. Loss of place

Knowing our place helps us feel safe. When we feel like we belong, we feel protected. Tribe has always meant protection from threats. It's a significant developmental leap when we learn the value of belonging and playing by the rules. Oxytocin, the love and trust biochemical, reinforces these pro-social behaviours.

Gemma has a strong need to belong, so she initiates ideas to create stronger bonds with the new team. When denied this intimacy she is deeply wounded, and feels unsafe, adrift.

'Belonging' can be blinding. Worrying about our place within a group can distract us from seeing how we are impacting others. When we are caught up in needing to feel included, we get needy and sulk. We seek approval and validation from others. 'Belonging' is a false sense of safety. Being part of a group assures nothing. It is better to turn inwards and find solace within, to know that one belongs to oneself, and as such belongs to the whole of humanity.

In the meantime, the primal need to belong, and the fear of losing the oxytocin and its sense of safety, can trigger the survival mechanism and give rise to one of the Four Devils.

4. Loss of performance

Dopamine is one of the reasons we get up and get going. It feels good to do something, to achieve something. Our work gives us the opportunity to achieve and experience dopamine, and then get rewarded for it through recognition and promotions, and the lovely serotonin we get on the back of that. Threats to our performance can trigger fear of losing both those opportunities: dopamine and serotonin.

Here's the thing that we need to know: performance is about process, not product. One of the challenges we have in workplaces is that we often believe the opposite – that performance is about results. This is true to a certain extent. We are always seeking outcomes.

The challenge lies when we get attached to the process for these outcomes. This is why we may become change-resistant. We think that the only way to produce results is the way we know already. A change of process creates a threat to our results, therefore a threat to our rewards are often attached.

Many of us attribute our worth and success to our ability to produce results. If something threatens our ability to produce results, we can become overwhelmed and feel threatened. Burnout can be a real threat as we overwork to keep pace with expectations around performance.

Our true value is not as producers, but as learners. When we can try new things and adapt our approach to new circumstances, then we can continue to be of service, we can continue to be contributors. Again, our worth is integral, not external. Yet our primal craving for dopamine can interfere with our more subtle insights.

Let's rewrite our Boardroom case study from a different point of view and see what biochemicals might be at play.

Peter, CEO: With title and positional authority, his serotonin is assured. The tension in the team threatens the oxytocin and dopamine he had worked hard to create with a high-performing team. Self-doubt puts all this at risk.

Stanley, Head of Corporate Services: Gemma's suggestions are perceived threats to his status, authority, and power. He is primed for an amygdala response.

Gemma, Head of Client Service: As a new team member, she is seeking a place within the group to secure oxytocin. She wants to prove her worth to gain status and serotonin, and she wants to progress some results to get some dopamine. With resistance to her efforts, she is threatened on multiple sides.

David, Chief Information Officer. As a quiet achiever, he enjoys harmony (oxytocin). His assessment of treatment of Gemma as unfair triggers threats to oxytocin and serotonin.

Stephanie, Head of Marketing: Concerned with group harmony and the power dynamics, Stephanie fears loss of both oxytocin and serotonin.

The characters are all primed for fear of loss of some type. These threats can trigger us, and those around us, into unhelpful behaviours I call the Four Devils. Let's meet them.

The Four Devils

It's important to name these people stuff issues as the Four Devils, or caricatures of what we experience. The reason why we must do this is two-fold:

1. We are reminded that we are more than what we see and hear. It reminds us that we are not our thoughts, we are not our feelings, we are not what we say, and we are not what we do. These are but manifestations of inner turmoil, not our core being. These caricatures remind us that the best version of ourself does not appear when we are driven by fear. We see unhelpful patterns of communication and behaviour that is driven by primal elements.

2. Once we see the pattern, we can change the pattern. Instead of getting caught up in our own stories, we can see the drivers that trigger the primal reactions. Once we see the patterns, it can act like a circuit breaker. We can then work on implementing new, more positive patterns.

Let's look at the Four Devils to see if we might understand them a little better, and then work our way towards dealing with them constructively. As we look at the Devils, we'll see them first in ourselves, before we deal with that same behaviour in others.

Devil 1: The Firebug

FIREBUG

BOARDROOM CASE STUDY

Turf wars and power issues

At the start of our story, Gemma had started a turf war with Stanley. In her keen desire to make a contribution and showcase her abilities, she stepped all over Stanley's toes. He reacted by calling out her territory infringements every chance he got.

BIG PICTURE

Firebug

Ever been so mad you couldn't shut up about it? Hello, Firebug. The Firebug happens when wind and fire ignite a firestorm. This is when fire (inner world of beliefs) combines with wind (outer expression of communication). Fear of loss of power is the spark.

The Firebug erupts when our beliefs are challenged. Negative thoughts combine with a need to be heard, and all of a sudden, someone sets the house on fire. Firebug issues centre around the primal fear of loss of power and autonomy. The people stuff problems that arise as a result are:

- Turf wars
- Conflict over ideas
- Power struggles
- Arguments
- Attention-seeking

As Firebugs, we have attitude problems. With perceived threats to our autonomy and status, we can feel apathetic, disgruntled, envious, and angry. In self-protection or in vengeance, we may then work to cause the downfall of others or a project. With calculating swipes, as a Firebug we aim to cause dissension so we can triumph as the savvy naysayer. As leaders, we always want to be mindful of when we are being triggered into Firebug territory. Noticing when we feel irate, then asking why, is the first step to unplugging from the trigger.

We want to shift the fear of loss of power to a love of learning. If we are being triggered to Firebug, we can stop and ask ourselves, 'What can I learn from this? How might this be an opportunity for growth?'

As a leader, if we are dealing with Firebugs in our team, we also want to shift them from lighting destructive conflicts to sparking inspiration. Where to start?

Start with perspective. If we look at Stanley and Gemma, why are there turf wars? Why are there power struggles? Why is there attention-seeking and argumentative behaviours? These behaviours are due to feeling insecure in their position. Power and control is the Firebug's false solution for trying to feel safe.

For Gemma, she needs a clear path to showcase her abilities, get recognition, and make a contribution. For Stanley, he needs to be reassured that he is still in charge of his area. Clarification of roles is a starting point.

If we are to use our skills of perspective, we also look at the underlying systems that might be contributing to this issue. What are the KPIs for each role? How are suggestions encouraged and processed as a group?

How is induction managed? Is there a process to help onboard new team members to help them feel secure in their role? How is power authorised in the group?

Lack of power creates resentment and resistance. No one likes to feel they have no autonomy. The solution? Build explicit scope of responsibilities and parameters so that team members can make decisions for themselves. There is nothing more time-consuming and belittling to a team member than having to check everything by the boss.

To defuse power games and move to shared power, we need to work with staff to give up our need to control. This is possible when we see our colleagues and competitors with love instead of fear. As leaders, we need to reassure our people where they have autonomy, where they have agency, and what power they can exercise. Feeling powerless can bring on the Firebug. Getting clear on roles and responsibilities is a great way to give people certainty and boundaries, and therefore grant people agency over their own decisions and actions.

The energy of transmuted power (energy that is focused on learning instead of control and power) allows constructive discontent and productive disagreement. We respect our colleagues and seek their contribution rather than stifling it. This is how we can expand results as a whole.

Distribute power, defuse tension

When people have an opportunity to exercise power in their world, there is less competitive tension. This requires the leader to make explicit what decisions can be made by whom, and then to outline the parameters with them. One of the leader's main roles here is to teach their team members *how* to make decisions. We do this by sharing what questions to ask and what factors to consider when looking at repercussions. This is how we help our team members develop judgment.

More than anything, people want to feel consulted and considered in any decision-making process. One of the sure-fire ways to activate the

Firebug within is to announce a decision without prior discussion with the people affected. It makes people feel powerless and disrespected. It rattles the power cage where our sense of autonomy feels trapped.

BRASS TACKS

How to turn a Firebug into a leader who sparks inspiration

1. Create clear boundaries

- Create parameters or guidelines clearly articulated for each team member
- Identify roles
- Identify responsibilities
- Agree on outcomes and timelines
- Create a check-in schedule
- Troubleshoot confusion zones
- Create a charter of agreed acceptable and non-acceptable behaviours
- Draft a manifesto with the team about their collective beliefs and intentions
- Schedule a review of the charter and manifesto and complete it.

2. Clarify decision-making processes

- Create a scope for individual decision-making: who can decide what, with which limits and constraints
- Wherever possible, encourage parties to resolve any issues between themselves using a conversation framework (this concept is introduced in *Loyalty*)
- Articulate and document a complaints process
- Articulate and document a conflict resolution process.

3. Delegate authority

- Identify what authority each individual has within the scope of their role. This might include purchasing responsibility, expense sign off, leave approval, hiring, promotions
- Together identify the criteria and constraints for each delegated responsibility
- Clarify areas over which they do **not** have delegated authority.

Transparency goes a long way in calming the Firebug. The more we can clarify process and decision-making, the more assured we will feel about our place and power within a group.

Devil 2: The Storm Driver

STORM DRIVER

BOARDROOM CASE STUDY

Fairness makes us fierce

David, the Chief Information Officer, saw what was happening to new recruit Gemma and thought it was distinctly unfair. She was only new, deserved a chance to prove herself, and definitely deserved to be treated better. Always one to fight for the underdog, David grew more and more angry. His emotions blew strong and hard. When people are triggered by a sense of fairness on behalf of others, the argument can become an emotional one of principles.

BIG PICTURE

Storm Driver

Storm Driver: When water and wind unleash a tempest. When water (inner world of emotions) combines with wind (outer expression of communication), we have emotional tirades. Loss of place, status and a sense of fairness stirs these elements.

Storm Drivers arise when our emotions are triggered. The need to be heard (wind) stirs emotional reactions (water), and all of a sudden we become an intense and active critic. Storm Driver issues arise from the fear of loss of position relative to others, notably of status and fairness, which are integral to our sense of place and security within a group. If these are challenged, then we move into a survival stance. The people stuff problems that arise as a result are:

- Condescension
- Dismissiveness
- Passive-aggressive behaviours
- Bullying
- Rage and anger
- Criticism
- Pessimism
- Resistance to change

We notice the Storm Driver rising in ourselves when we're triggered into riding the high horse of justice. It's impossible to argue with us as we become single-minded in our pursuit of righteousness. We become blind to any arguments but our own. If we find ourselves digging into an argument, becoming even more attached to our point of view, it's time to stop, step back, and practice perspective. What point of view are we so attached to? How might others see it? What triggers are there for us personally?

As leaders, if we have Storm Drivers arise in our teams, we need to address issues of fairness and status and make sure each person feels they have been treated well. Radical transparency and consistent explanation of the 'why' behind decisions can help defuse some of the tension that arises from perceived threats to status and unfairness.

As leaders, we can help others to feel secure in their position by celebrating each other, acknowledging one another, and showing appreciation and encouragement. It can be a joyful experience.

BRASS TACKS

How to turn a Storm Driver into a leader who spreads passion

1. Explain decisions

- When we explain the process and reasoning behind a decision, it helps others see that due consideration was given in making the decision, including how it would affect others.

- Remind team members that their interests have been fairly represented and duly considered. They may not like the outcome, but they can come to appreciate and respect the process, if the process had been respectful towards them.

- Show compassion if the decision will have what might be considered a detrimental effect.

- Model how to shift perspective by inviting them to consider what opportunities there may be behind the disappointment.

2. Affirm positions

Changes in titles, office desk, and parking access all affect perceived status. Be sure to clarify where the person's standing is in the organisation and team.

Affirm the essential contribution the individual makes.

If relevant, signal status with delegated work, assignments, or consulting on projects/issues.

Identify a clear development path for each team member so they know they are appreciated and encouraged in their growth.

3. Acknowledge accomplishments

- Recognise a person's efforts and accomplishments publicly and privately in a manner meaningful to them.
- Show how the individual's contributions have led to team or organisational results. Highlight what they have done especially well and the impact it had on others.

When our obsession with position, status and fairness shifts and we feel stable in our relationships with others, we are more able to adopt a love of learning perspective. Mistakes and lessons are not seen as a status or fairness threat, but something to be embraced as they help us individually and collectively progress. If we are not hampered by the fear of missing out, we can instead be motivated to create more wealth and resources for more people. Instead of the constricting self-focus that chokes our focus and energy, we radiate possibilities with our broader scope. This is how we can help Storm Drivers spread passion instead of rage and anger.

If Peter takes the time to explain decisions, affirm positions, and acknowledge accomplishments, he might calm emotional concerns about fairness and status for Stanley and David. When people know they are being seen and recognised, fear and frustration diminish.

Devil 3: The Ground Splitter

BOARDROOM CASE STUDY
Closed door conversations

Head of marketing, Stephanie, sees herself as a do-gooder. Primed with good intentions, she sets about highlighting the shortcomings of her colleagues' behaviour, for the sake of the whole. She worries about the team's productivity and ability to meet their targets. She also worries that the situation will end up piling on more work for her. Rather than calling out the issues with the whole team, Stephanie works behind the scenes to get an outcome.

Stephanie decides the best way to approach the tension in the team is to do it privately with the CEO, instead of challenging the issues as a whole group. She shares her criticism with Peter, then pretends everything is fine with her peers. This kind of duplicitous action can be good or ill-intentioned: she may be doing her best to assist in conflict avoidance and resolution, or may also be working to shore up her relationship with the CEO in a bid for power and influence. The effect may appear inauthentic, and Stephanie runs the risk of being seen as two-faced.

BIG PICTURE
Ground Splitter

Ever been so swamped with work you just buried your head in the sand? So overloaded and stressed out that you complained behind the scenes about so-and-so instead of facing it head on? You might be saying hello to the Ground Splitter.

Ground Splitter: when the earth shakes and fires erupt from underground. Ground Splitters have behaviour problems. A negative and resistant mindset (fire – the inner experience of beliefs) wants an outlet and finds it in unhelpful actions (earth – the outer expression of behaviour). This can have a slow burn effect, or it can be more dramatic, like an earthquake with its explosive fires. The impact is divisive.

The people stuff problems that present include:

- Backbiting
- White anting
- Blank-faced reactions
- Two-faced interactions
- Silos
- Change resistance
- Hidden agendas
- Entitlement
- Shirking of responsibility
- Lack of urgency

When we turn into Ground Splitters, we are triggered by the fear of loss of performance and threats to productivity. We may disagree with decisions because we perceive we will be overworked as a result. We may default to silos to preserve our own priorities. Keep our heads down, bum up. Pedal to the metal. Going flat out. These are all images we conjure in Ground Splitter mode. The sense that we are being pushed to the very edge of our capacity: it threatens all our thresholds, and burnout is nigh. We feel unable to affect change through direct petitioning, and so resort to isolating ourselves in work, or undermining others. If we find ourselves defaulting to ground splitting behaviours, we need to stop and take a time out. We ask ourselves: 'What is triggering this unhelpful, reactive behaviour? Where can I exercise better influence? How can I be more open in my communication?'

If we experience Ground Splitters on our team, we feel like we have enemies everywhere. They can experience a rising sense of injustice coupled with powerlessness. Challenging authority is seen as an ineffective and dangerous way to affect change, so they lash out in small, underhanded ways to ease pain and frustration. Silos are a call for safety. People protect their patch when they feel threatened. Our job as leaders is to reduce uncertainty, provide clarity, and close any skills gap. We must avoid assuming people's behaviour is due to incompetence or poor attitude; this is not often the case.

In Ground Splitter mode, it is likely one or more of these dynamics are at play: maturity, emotional intelligence, and clear expectations.

Collaboration requires considerable leadership maturity. It needs individuals to feel grounded in their own ability as well as safe and supported to express contrary opinions. Collaboration means changing how we define ourselves and our roles. We need to drop the safety blanket of role and title and embrace collegiality and co-crafted results where we don't stand out but stand together. To be a co-creator and a collaborator requires huge growth in self-awareness. It requires the courage to make mistakes. It requires well-established norms and boundaries to make it safe to collaborate as well.

An emotional intelligence upgrade is needed. All humans are governed by their limbic (emotional) system. It trumps the rational part of the brain, the cortex, every time. Emotional intelligence skills help us see and monitor when emotions are wanting to drive the show, and they help us still the crazy beast. It's possible that negativity and undermining is a sign of underdeveloped emotional intelligence. Later we look at how to develop this in self and others.

Clear expectations are required. No one wants to micro-manage. We want to give the benefit of the doubt. With this good intention, we sometimes either fail to leave a clear enough picture or to coach others to find their own approach. So yes, our Ground Splitters probably need more explicit instructions.

BRASS TACKS

How to turn a Ground Splitter into a leader who sows purpose

As leaders, we need to model what effective work looks like. We need to be mindful of when we leave work at the end of the day, how we manage our own stress levels and our stress relief. We need to keep iterating what is expected, what is not appropriate (when it comes to overwork), and what we value in others.

1. Define success and measure progress

Success is more than just completing tasks. Success is about creating positive outcomes for the people we aim to serve. Part of the reason we may feel overwhelmed with work is that we may have lost sight of our purpose and how we define success, and have become obsessed with our task list. If we ask instead: "how is this helping us serve others better/faster/easier?" it shifts our focus away from our immediate deliverables towards our long-term objective.

- Define success. Include process success (e.g. we solve problems together) as well as outcomes.
- Clarify purpose. Make sure everyone can answer this: "what are we really here to do?"
- Measure progress.
- Measure activity that we know produces results, as well as the results in themselves. Most leaders measure the wrong thing: they focus on lag measures instead of the results that lead towards it.

This is how we change the focus and the conversation. It becomes less about *doing* stuff, and more about doing the *right stuff* – the stuff that leads to the outcome we desire.

2. Close the skills gap

One of the reasons that people retreat to silos is that they are hanging on to what they know. It's a defensive and protective measure. If we are asking people to step up, we are often asking them to try things they have never done before. We may not have prepared them effectively for this new activity.

- Create a 'safe to fail/safe to try' culture.
- Give them the skills and training required for the activity we want them to take on.
- Give them technical skills and people stuff skills.
- Establish where they are in their leadership maturity. What perspective and capacities do they need next?

3. Create team accountability

- Create team KPIs. One of the big failures in organisations is having individual KPIs only. An organisation is a dynamic system that all staff operate within, contribute to, and are affected by. We need to create team accountability, not just individual ones. This stops lone wolf behaviour, as well as silos. The more we can help people to see how interconnected our work is, the more we will drop the barriers that keep us from collaborating and connecting.
- Ask the team how they want to be held accountable. Ask them what should happen if we miss targets and deadlines. How should the group handle it?
- Run pre- and postmortems. Pre-mortems troubleshoot what could go wrong, and then take steps to mitigate these challenges. Postmortems look at what did go wrong (and right) so the team can learn from it.

One of the reasons people become two-faced is that there may not be good processes in place to raise issues. People may not feel safe to do so. In addition to feeling swamped by overwork, they may feel powerless and scared to raise issues. Grumblings and manoeuvring behind the scenes may seem like the only viable option.

When we look behind the narrow constraints of performance and see the outcomes we are striving for, and the people we aim to help, we realise that we are all working towards something bigger than ourselves. We begin to sow purpose.

When we sow purpose and drop the fear of underperforming, we can experience a new energy. We feel gratitude. We can develop a common agenda. We find it much easier to collaborate. We take initiative and encourage others to do so as well. Together we drive change, not resist it.

Devil 4: The Water Bomber

BOARDROOM CASE STUDY

Untamed emotions

Newcomer Gemma is at the whim of her emotions. Wanting to make a contribution, challenged by Stanley, she is overwhelmed by insecurity. She feels alone and unsupported in a workplace she does not yet understand. Her emotional overflow is unrelenting and starts to alienate others, making her feel even more alone. It's a negative reinforcing loop that leaves her feeling worse and worse.

Her lack of emotional control and ineffective expression of it makes her a prime target of avoidance as her emotional ups and downs leak all over others. She is primarily affected by the sense of exclusion and lack of appreciation she is experiencing. She feels unsafe and lonely in the workplace as a result, which diminishes her productivity and engagement.

Peter the CEO is another version of the Water Bomber: he retreats and isolates as his own inner narrative creates a cesspool of self-doubt. Both are difficult to engage with.

BIG PICTURE

Water Bomber

Ever been caught up in your emotional drama? Ever been so immersed in the story you just can't see anything else? Say hello to your Water Bomber.

Water Bomber: when water hurls against the earth, it leaves a mess. When water (our inner experience of emotions) washes against the earth (our outer expression of behaviour), we can be a destructive flood, dragging others into our wake. The trigger for this maelstrom is fear of loss of place. Belonging is threatened.

When we fall into Water Bomber, it's because we are triggered by overwhelming emotions. Unrestrained emotional reactions (water) are expressed through unhelpful behaviours (earth). When we become Water Bombers, we leave an energetic wake in our path that soaks all around us. We can be a tsunami of yuck.

As Water Bombers, we are pushed around by our emotions. We might shut down, ruminate, sulk, or be reactive and volatile.

Water Bomber issues are triggered by the fear of loss of place within a group. Specifically, belonging, appreciation, and recognition feature in Water Bomber concerns. They cut straight to a person's sense of safety. Belonging is one of the most primal needs for tribal animals like humans. We have survived millennia because of belonging to groups. If our belonging in a group is threatened, our very sense of survival is threatened too. The people stuff problems when we are triggered into Water Bomber include:

- Blaming
- Sulking
- Presenteeism
- Jealousy
- Lack of self-reflection
- Lack of engagement

- Weeping and sobbing
- Shutting down and isolating

When we are triggered into Water Bomber, it is difficult to console us as we feel vulnerable and find it difficult to feel safe or trust others. We can become immersed in our emotional world of pain and have difficulty finding a rational perspective.

Few of us have been taught emotional resilience skills. If we've been lucky, we've had them modelled by leaders or family members. If we're resourceful, we might seek out these skills ourselves after being confronted by a difficult experience. I've dedicated a whole section to developing these emotional competencies, coming up next.

In the meantime, when we as leaders are dealing with a Water Bomber, we need to focus on three skills: awareness, attention, and anticipation. Awareness is bringing attention to the emotions people are experiencing and the impact they are having on others. This is where our feedback and coaching skills come into play. Attention is encouraging constructive attention to possibilities instead of problems. We can help guide our Water Bomber to focus there. Anticipation is the gentle encouragement of forward focus, of what could be good, and what they might be able to do next.

When we stop obsessing about our place and whether we are being recognised or appreciated, we can shift our attention to what really matters: helping one another and being in service to our mission. By bringing awareness and attention to the emotions at play we can help release their grip on us. With gentle prompting, we can steer attention to anticipation. What we can do next and what positive experiences we can create together. When we feel safe in our environment, we can be open to growth and develop a love of learning. This is how we can start to grow focus on what matters most, and what feels the best.

When we are not so worried about ourselves and allow love for others to flow, we enable trust and support. We include others instead of worrying about if we ourselves are included. We discover new determination and resilience.

BRASS TACKS

How to turn a Water Bomber into a leader who grows focus

To deal with threats to sense of place and belonging, we need to emphasise membership in community. All workplaces are mini-communities, and as leaders we need to foster the sense of belonging as a result.

1. Create symbols and rituals

We know we belong when we are part of common practices and have the emblems of the group. These create shapes and signals that we are part of something bigger than ourselves. From a leadership maturity point of view, this speaks to first our emerging awareness that we are stronger together, that we are not alone, and that there is safety in numbers. So, as leaders we can shape this experience with others.

- Name the group or the team.
- Get everyone the same pen or mug or mousepad or t-shirt.
- Have regular standing meetings, or walking meetings, or check-ins, or Friday Frappes, or whatever creates a cadence of interactions. For more details, you can read more in my book, Loyalty.

2. Show appreciation

When we are appreciated, we get a rush of oxytocin and serotonin. Oxytocin is the feel-good neurotransmitter that signals feeling safe and loved. Serotonin is the neurotransmitter for self-esteem and wellbeing. Oxytocin and serotonin also help boost the immune system. Appreciation is a powerful elixir for building team harmony and engagement.

- Say thank you.
- Catch them doing something right, and tell them.
- Tell them how their work has had a positive impact on you or others.

3. Recognise achievements

When we feel recognised, we experience a surge of serotonin. This neurotransmitter is responsible for esteem and sense of wellbeing. When we see others getting recognised, we have the same experience – a serotonin rush. Recognition can take many forms, both public and private. Find out what your team members value most and serve up the recognition in a way that they appreciate.

- Recognise someone's achievements one-to-one, privately.
- Recognise group and individual achievements publicly.
- Mark milestones in a project, organisation or career.
- Find something to celebrate and do so often.

As leaders, our role is to craft a sense of belonging and a sense of place within the group. We can create group norms and rituals and invite others to participate alongside us. Togetherness triumphs over emotional storms.

Developing emotional competency in self and others

The Four Devils, just like the shadow archetypes, are not the best version of ourselves. Like the archetypes, these have triggers that release unhelpful behaviours and attitudes, making us difficult to deal with.

The critical antidote for these triggers is deep self-mastery and awareness. This is understanding how our beliefs and emotions feed one another, in negative or positive reinforcing loops. In this section, we will explore emotional mastery techniques as well as common belief traps.

When it comes to sharing feelings, leaders have mixed reactions. Many feel emotions have no place in the workplace, and distract from getting on with the job. Secretly they fear being seen as weak if they acknowledge emotional responses. Others believe that laying it all out there is being authentic and genuine.

While being stoic can be seen as cold and aloof, being overly emotional can also be distressing. Untempered emotions are like ripping off scabs that bleed all over others. Most people are not equipped to handle their own emotional disturbance, let alone that of others. Some emotional divulgences can even trigger flashbacks and unease in those around us. It is one of the reasons we feel uncomfortable around people who have meltdowns and crying episodes. We simply don't know how to handle it. Unfettered emotions are expressions of the Four Devils.

As a society, we have not yet included deep emotional competence as a critical social skill to be taught and nurtured. Most of us are not taught how to feel our feelings fully, in a useful and constructive way. We are told to bury them, to pull our socks up and soldier on. The alternative to steely reserve and its counterpoint of messy emotions, is to be *real* rather than *raw*. Being raw is about being an open book, completely transparent, in all of our jiggling messiness. It's compelling, kind of like watching open heart surgery. Fascinating and revolting at the same time. Being real is the ability to experience one's emotions fully, to have emotions, and not be them. It's about being open, but not so much that we ooze and gush over others. Being real is more like an X-Ray than surgery. You can see everything that is going on without getting dirty.

Learning to experience and express feelings without being carried away by them is a missing critical leadership skill – the skill of being real.

How to develop the skills of being real (in ourselves and others)

These processes are also tools in perspective; how we see and experience our emotions and thoughts. The perspective skill is that of seeing ourselves as an object to study, and we learn to play witness to our emotional experiences. Let's take a look at how we can use perspective to give us better emotional awareness and management.

There are three areas of focus for developing emotional agility: body, brain, and language.

1. Body focus

Being aware of emotions is essential to developing our self-awareness. It starts by paying attention to the body, and what we are experiencing in it. Emotions are simply energy in the body. When we feel anxious, we may experience this as a sensation somewhere in the body. For me, I will feel my throat constrict. Others feel a tension headache, or a pressure in the chest. This is simply energy being produced in the body in response to our inner dialogue and stories.

By using awareness for pinpointing where we are experiencing emotions in the body, we can then move to regulation of that emotion. The 'regulation' component is both a passive and active approach. In the active regulation of emotion, we simply move. We can exercise, stretch, shift position, get outside, stand up straight, even yell or cry. We move energy through the body rather than let it stagnate in an emotional well.

Passive regulation occurs simply by observing the emotions. We take a witnessing perspective. Observe the emotions. Use imagination to identify a shape, colour, texture, moment, or temperature of the emotion. Breathe and observe. This act of neutral observation acts as a pressure valve and releases some of the emotional tension. It does not eliminate the cause of the emotional trigger, but simply allows the swirling emotional energy to dissipate and give us a better chance of getting back in the driver's seat.

> **Body focus skills to practice:**
>
> *Body scan.* Each morning, do a body scan. How does your body feel? Are there parts that feel tense or uncomfortable? Imagine breathing ease into those parts.
>
> *Movement.* Incorporate a movement regime in your day. Any type of exercise will do, from stretching through to weight training and running. As you do your movements, pay attention to how the body feels.
>
> *Label your emotions.* Go for subtle distinctions in the feelings, not just 'good' or 'happy.' You might feel 'amused' or 'content'.
>
> *Practise locating emotions in the body.* Use your imagination to notice colour, shape, texture, temperature.

2. Brain focus

Being able to notice emotions requires the ability to focus. In *Leadership is Upside Down* (2014), this is quoted as 'brain integration' by neuroscientists Harald S. Harung and Frederick Travis.[18] Brain integration has three measures:

1. The level of coherence in the different areas of the executive part of the brain.
2. Quicker access to the alpha brain wave state (attention to one's inner state of well-being).
3. A better match of brain activation and task demands.

They say people who have better brain integration have higher emotional stability, decreased anxiety, and are more open to new experiences. In other words, if we can master our brain state, we can better manage our emotional state.

According to Harung and Travis, there are three key elements that seem to characterise someone whose brain is powerful and effective:

1. The ability to focus on a task, tuning out distractions and interruptions.

---

[18] Damiano, S. *Leadership is Upside Down: The i4 Neuroleadership Revolution*

2. The capacity to adapt in exceptional ways to harness the process of neuroplasticity (basically the brain changing itself over time).
3. The ability to sustain effort over time (meaning never giving up, even when the task may be difficult).

The best way to develop brain integration and effectiveness?

Meditation and mindfulness.

What? You expected something different? This has been the go-to most effective method of developing focus used over thousands of years by numerous wise and compassionate leaders. Both meditation and mindfulness are the practice of focus. In meditation, we draw our attention to a singular thing, such as the breath, a mantra, or an object like candle. In mindfulness, we hone awareness and focus by opening our senses to the exquisite detail of things around us through all our senses. Both practices require exclusive focus on the present moment, the here and now.

In practising both mindfulness and meditation, we find that we grow calmer. We notice more easily when our emotions are triggered and can then pull back from the Four Devils taking over. We remain firmly in the driver's seat, while we can observe our emotions, in the passenger seat.

Brain focus skills to practice:

Meditation: For 5-20 minutes each day, practice closing your eyes and paying attention to your breath. If your mind wanders, just bring your attention back gently to the breath.

Mindfulness: For a meal, or over a cup of coffee or tea, pay detailed attention to the sensations you are experiencing. From taste, smell, colour, textures, sounds. Just immerse yourself in the deliciousness of the experience.

3. Language focus

Language is a gateway to emotions. When we can label our emotions, we ease their grip on us. When we can talk about them, they come apart from us. They become an experience we have, rather than an identity we adopt. Language can ramp up emotions or calm them down. How we describe something can transform an incident from a devastation to a distraction. Pictures are transformed into a story with multiple paths to the past and ones to the future too. The art of the writer is to craft vivid pictures to help transport you. This is great in fiction, not so great when toe-to-toe with people in real life.

Take this story of a parent and child:

Parent: "How was your day?"

Child: "It was the worst day ever! I could have died from embarrassment! My teacher is the cruellest person alive! I hate everyone and everything!"

We call it 'drama' for a reason. This kind of emotive language stirs passion and presses our emotions into overdrive. We can also use language to de-identify emotions: 'I am experiencing frustration' versus 'I am frustrated'. When we use 'I am' we become whatever comes after that word. If it's emotions, we literally become that emotion: angry, sad, devastated. This is how we put emotions in the driver's seat. When we use 'I am experiencing this emotion', we acknowledge emotions are along for the ride. Definitely not in control.

We are meaning-making machines. Events are neutral. We create stories that translate them, and those make us feel good or bad. If we are to take control of our inner world, we need to take control of the inner narrative. We need to change the stories we tell about the experiences we have.

In his fabulous book, *Extreme Ownership: How U.S. Navy SEALS Lead and Win*, former US Navy SEAL Jocko Willinck (2015) says he has one response to all events: "Good." No matter what happens, that is how he responds. It's his circuit breaker to look for the opportunity, and not get stuck in the fear of loss. It's a great pivot. It takes discipline to practice this consistently.

Try it:

- 'COVID-19 has shut down your business indefinitely'. Good. I can now work on cleaning my house and do some big picture thinking.
- 'The bushfires wiped out your home and everything you own.' Good. I can now practise minimalism.
- 'You have cancer.' Good. I can now slow down and do some more meditation.
- 'Your mother died.' Good. She is no longer in pain.

Like I said, it's a disciplined practice. And effective. Control awareness and attention, not emotions.

> *"The limits of my language mean the limits of my world."*
> *– Ludwig Wittgenstein*

Language focus skills to practice:

'Everything is good' journal exercise: At the end of each day, make a list of three things that happened. Just list the facts. Then write, 'this was good because ..."

Practice exaggeration: Pick something ordinary from your daily experience, like checking the mailbox. Now practice interpreting that experience through an exaggeration lens by using 'it was the BEST THING EVER because ...' or 'it was the WORST THING EVER because ... As a bonus, notice when you use exaggeration like this in your conversations, and the effect it has on your emotional life.

Refection on personal stories: Think about the stories you tell about yourself to others. It might be about your family, about your upbringing, your work, or something significant that has happened to you, like a divorce or a trip around the globe. What interpretation do you give when you tell these stories? Was it good? Was it bad? Has it made a lasting difference? Was it a turning point? Notice how these stories make you feel as a result.

BRASS TACKS

How to tackle the Four Devils in your leadership

The tough work of people stuff in leadership is when we are dealing with communication and behaviour that is challenging and unproductive.

1. Understand drivers

The first step to dealing with it is to try and understand its drivers. No one goes out of their way deliberately to be nasty or undermining. The causes stem from survival reactions from a fear of loss that include:

- Loss of power
- Loss of position relative to others
- Loss of place within a group
- Loss of performance.

2. Deal with behaviour and communicate with feedback

To deal with these issues, we need to first address the problematic behaviours and interactions. No matter how understandable the cause is, the effect on others needs to be redressed. We do this by providing feedback and encouraging self-awareness around the impact of behaviour and emotions on others.

3. Redress the causes of turbulence

Power

- Create clear boundaries
- Clarify decision-making process
- Delegate authority.

Position

These are about fairness and status issues and feeling powerless. These reassurances will help move from fear of losing position to spreading passion.

- Explain decisions
- Affirm position
- Acknowledge accomplishments.

Place
- Create symbols and rituals
- Show appreciation
- Recognise achievements.

Performance
- Define success and measure progress
- Close the skills gap
- Create team accountability.

When we have people stuff issues to deal with, we need to remember that there are triggers that cause the problems. These triggers are integrated in our biochemistry, and we seek the feel-good effect of dopamine, serotonin, endorphins, and oxytocin. Fear of their loss spikes cortisol and can prompt an amygdala hijack. As leaders, we first need to be mindful of our own triggers and to develop the emotional agility to control our focus and stay centred. When we lead others who are triggered, we can help guide them back to an even keel while addressing the broader conditions that are provoking their biochemistry.

Is there a way back for our crew under Peter's leadership? Absolutely. All teams can recover from culture breakdowns like these ones. The best chance of success comes when the CEO leads the turnaround. It requires deep self-awareness and a boatload of courage and support. Re-establishing rapport and trust takes concerted effort, with plenty of frank and difficult conversations. No doubt about it, leadership is hard.

It's a lot to manage: being aware of our triggers, the pull to the shadow archetypes, and the conditions that cause the Four Devils. This is the work of wise and compassionate leaders! This is the work we need to do if we are to handle the complex challenges ahead as a collective.

PART FIVE

US

Perspective on the bigger things

Our leadership context has evolved in stunning ways while our biochemistry has not. In the previous sections, we looked at the practice of perspective to help us develop a broad and encompassing point of view while also honing our skills to be both sensitive and sensible. We looked at how we see ourselves as leaders and which archetypes might serve us well as we navigate business. We highlighted the traps that come with each of these archetypes that can pull us away from our mission to be wise and compassionate. Then we explored the troublesome people stuff that arises in the form of the Four Devils and how we can manage our emotions and conditions to tame these Devils. These are fundamentals that are not going away, even as our world tilts a little on its axis with the complex and volatile challenges we face.

We come now to what's next. If we master the people stuff when it comes to ourselves and the people around us, how can we then lean into serving the broader picture of Us? Let's take a look.

BOARDROOM CASE STUDY

A view from afar

Rusty Schweickart felt sick. It was March 1969 and he was on the Apollo 9 space mission, attempting the very first extravehicular activity (EVA) in space. His nausea is called 'space adaptation syndrome' and about half of space travellers experience it. It's the opposite of motion sickness – the person and object appear to be in relative motion but there is no corresponding sensation in the body and inner ear. The brain has trouble reconciling the sensations, and the strong urge to vomit takes over.

Rusty recovered enough to undertake a limited version of the EVA and to test the portable life support system (which was used by the following twelve astronauts who walked on the Moon).

During a five-minute pause during his EVA, he looked down on the earth, considering its place in the universe. As he stared at our planet, he underwent a metaphysical experience, sensing the interconnectedness of all things. The universe was a profoundly connected entity. Apollo 14 astronaut Edgar Schein describes the emotion as 'interconnected euphoria'. As with many other astronauts, it changed his perspective forever. On his return to earth, he started practising transcendental meditation. He continued his work at NASA and remained committed to space exploration.

Rusty reflects: "We're not passengers on Spaceship Earth. We're the crew."

His experience changed his sense of responsibility for the planet.

Rusty is not alone in his experience. Many astronauts report similar shifts in perspective. In his book The *Cosma Hypothesis: Implications of the Overview Effect* (2018), author Frank White calls this the 'overview effect'. He describes it as a cognitive shift in awareness. The experience of seeing the planet first-hand against the vast emptiness of space reinforces a sense of its fragility and uniqueness. All the diverse miracles of life wrapped by a thin atmosphere hurtling through space captures a sense of responsibility. From space there are no borders, no countries, no politics. The need to become a planetary society united in the protection of our pale blue dot becomes an essential and obvious imperative.

Since not all of us will have the opportunity to see Earth from space, scientists have pushed to recreate the experience, including a children's program called SpaceBuzz launched by the European Space Agency (ESA), the Overview Effect Foundation, and the Netherlands Space Office,[19] as well as a University of Missouri research project that aimed to reproduce the overview effect through a virtual reality headset, an isolation tank and half a tonne of Epsom salts intended to create "instant global consciousness."[20]

Another astronaut Ron Garan describes not only a shift of perspective, but a call to action. He calls this the Orbital Perspective.[21] He says that in our aim to simplify and make sense of the complexity of our human systems, we reduce people to categories. We put up walls and barriers. We judge and separate. When we see the world from space, we have a new perspective: one where we are all in this together. 'Home' is defined not as a country or a city or neighbourhood, but as the whole planet itself. Through his experience working on the International Space Station, Garan has experienced first-hand the ability to collaborate to solve problems. He sees that we are all in this together, we are all interconnected, and we are planetary citizens with a responsibility to innovate and create solutions together for the long term, multi-generational future.

So, how is this useful for you?

When your child comes screaming to you because their sibling has stolen their *Frozen* lunchbox, or when your spouse nags you to fold the laundry, or when your staff member interrupts yet again with 'have you got a minute …?'

We are far from the bliss of interconnected euphoria.

And yet, if some part of us can remain tethered to this awareness, like Rusty looped to his spacecraft looking down on the planet, then we can become so much more down-to-earth. We can remember that life is at once temporary and endless, painful and full of joy. We can take everything in our stride, smile through chaos, and savour all of it. And get down to work.

---

19   Read more about the program here: www.spacebuzz.earth/
20   Sample, I. (26 Dec 2019). Scientists attempt to recreate 'overview effect' from Earth.
21   Garan, R. (Feb 10, 2015). The Orbital Perspective.

BIG PICTURE

Perspective on us

As I wrote this book, humanity is facing a once in a 100-year event: the COVID-19 pandemic. More than any other event in the modern age, more than either of the World Wars, this health crisis is creating a shared experience across borders and oceans. The virus does not discriminate.

This is what the experience is revealing to us:

Our interconnection is one of our greatest strengths as a species. It is also one of our biggest weaknesses. What affects one affects us all.

There is a gift in that realisation: we are truly only as strong as our weakest member. Our most vulnerable individuals are also our biggest collective vulnerability. The elderly, remote communities, Indigenous people, and homeless are all the most at risk. Consider how homeless people, who do not have the resources to shelter or clean themselves, are more susceptible to contracting and therefore spreading COVID-19. If only we can help them to be safe and clean in their own space then we would eliminate a possible germ bomb detonating once again. I'm aware this sounds like self-interest dressed up as compassion. In my view, if it takes the basic personal survival instinct to generate compassionate action towards our fellow human beings, no matter the underlying motivation, then this is a good thing. Take care of our weaker members and we all grow stronger.

As the world economies grind to a halt and stumble with falling stock prices and rising unemployment, we see also the vulnerabilities of our capitalist system. The immutable law of supply and demand is strangled by forced shut-downs and quarantine orders. Our health affects our wealth, just as our wealth affects our health. We see clearly how government, trade, health and education are in a symbiotic relationship with one another. There are thresholds and pressure points.

For example in Walker and Salt's *Resilience Thinking* (2006), when a system is interrupted with excessive inputs or outputs, there is a point reached where the system's established balancing mechanisms reach breaking point and the whole system collapses. The good news is that it just doesn't dissolve completely. A new system emerges, with new dynamics, relationships, feedback loops and interplay of inputs and outputs.

This is where we are right now: thresholds are being tested. We are about to burst the banks of our economic, political, health, government, and educational systems. People have lost their jobs and livelihoods. Many people have died and are dying. The health system is straining to cope. The government is supplying cash bailouts to keep the economy on life support.

Something new is likely to emerge.

It's much better if we get deliberate and conscious about it. This is absolutely where we need the power of perspective. We need to have the biggest and widest view possible. We need to see all of Us, all of humanity, all living things, on this one tiny blue dot, working together for something good.

We need the wisdom and compassion of the Elder. We need the courage of the Warrior. The stoic steadiness of the Diplomat. The ferocious tenacity of the Guardian to protect what is best of our humanity and traditions. The imagination and daring of the Pioneer to chart a course through unknown waters, strewn with the detritus of our past shipwrecks.

We are emergent.

Where do we start?

We start with the practice of perspective. Zoom out and expand to see generations past and generations forward. Zoom in to see what's next. Distil the best options. Discern who and where we can start to assist. Apply wisdom and compassion to any options.

The way forward is unclear. We need a rallying cry to keep us from losing our way.

Make a Declaration

In my interview with leadership coach Barry Pogorel, we explored how we lead transformation through uncertainty.[22] I first asked him how we can craft a vision for a better future where we can invent new modes of being and thinking and working.

He said: "Make a Declaration. Like the *Declaration of Human Rights*. Back then the founders of the US did not know what a democratic country could look like. They just knew that they wanted to stand for something: freedom from monarchy and the actualisation of self-government. There was a whole lot of detail to work out, but they knew that was the fundamental principle on which they would craft the future of the country's political, social, and economic systems. As the Civil War threatened much of those early ideals, they almost didn't make it."

Today, the pandemic is challenging us again. It may in fact be time for a new Declaration. Not just for the United States, but for the world as a whole. Now that we have ground our economic and political and social systems to a halt, what might we create next? How do we craft a new Declaration?

The intersection of People, Planet, and Place reveals where we can roll up our sleeves and dig in.

Three spheres of concern in your Declaration

As we ponder what our collective and personal Declarations might look like, we can consider three important interconnected spheres:

1. People: What affects one affects us all. How we treat our most vulnerable is what we invite for each of us. The pandemic has shown us what the mystics and philosophers have been saying for millennia: what we do and how we behave affects the webs between us.

2. Planet: We need to be symbionts, not parasites. We have long thought of the earth as a resource to be exploited. We need to live in a conscious way that does not deplete the natural ecosystem beyond

---

22 Listen to the interview on the podcast page at zoerouth.com

our repair. When we live more harmoniously with our natural world, all can thrive.

3. Place: Make the built environment beautiful. As a species, we have survived and thrived through the construction of built environments for accommodation, organisation, recreation, and representation. A considered approach to the built environment can promote beauty and enhance goodness.

As we redefine who and what we include in our sphere of Us and make a declaration for the brave new world we are to create, we come back to the here and now. To the people we have in front of us, to the leader we are right now. We can be simultaneously inspired by the emerging vision and dwarfed by it. We are small in the sea of humanity. The problems are huge. Does our work really make a difference?

Just like a single cell seems expendable in the human body, we too can feel insignificant. And yet, in linking with others, cells form tissues, form organs, create complex systems, and manifest as a magnificent human body. People gather and we become the fabric of humanity. What we do as individuals contributes to the health as a whole. We may not always see it or feel it, but we do matter. Our work with people stuff matters. If we can mend relationships, if we can encourage wisdom and compassion, then we are making a worthy contribution.

We are not alone, and we are better together.

BRASS TACKS

Leading for Us

Expand perspective. How far can you reach in to the past and future? How far can you extend your impact? Who else can you include in your sphere of concern and influence?

Make a declaration. What kind of world do you wish to live and work in? What principle and values do you want to live by? How might you make a contribution to people, planet, and place?

Join with others. Bring your vision to life by sharing it with others; your family, friends, colleagues, and staff. Join a community to help bring this vision to life with inspiration and accountability.

CONCLUSION

My promise to you in this book was that if you could see better, you could lead better. How did we do?

There is much to look at! From the grand spectrum of time and generations through to primitive biochemistry, human interactions are complex and far reaching. There are traps hiding everywhere. Even in choosing archetypes to help guide our actions, we can fall victim to a failure of perspective. If we let our focus turn inwards to selfish concerns, the shadow emerges. When we witness the Four Devils, the peril is to judge others for their behaviour. We blame the challenges on personalities, rather than dig a little deeper to the biochemical triggers and the systems that sparked them.

Even when we lift our gaze to the world in which we live, it is all too easy to turn away again, feeling helpless and insignificant.

Responsibility of leadership has always been heavy. When we expand the ripples of impact outwards through perspective, it can feel onerous. Leadership is also a privilege and a joy. We can learn! We can grow! We can help others! We can achieve! We can contribute!

In *People Stuff*, my wish is that you have tools for honing insight and skills to practice sensible and sensitive leadership. It is in your head, heart and hands now. It's up to you to take the next best actions. I wish you courage and strength.

And you don't have to do it alone.

Leadership is a collective practice. It is not done in isolation. (Though it can be done throughout 'isolation', as during the COVID-19 lockdown). Leadership happens with others, through others, and for others. Why then get stuck feeling you are alone?

All leaders need a posse. It's here we can test our perspective. It's here we can grind away rough edges with 'tough love' feedback from supportive peers. It's here we can express our feelings without judgment, to show up real, and be renewed. If we are to master people stuff, we need people. Our posse people.

How do you find such a posse pod?

Create your own pod. Reach out to leaders you admire in your industry and out, and suggest a get-together. To share challenges. To recommend resources. Even just to catch up and have a yarn (a chat, for non-Aussie readers!).

Join a pod

There are plenty of formal groups supporting leaders. A quick Google search will reveal local and international options.

Join my pod

The leaders I work with are a humble lot. They have one thing in common: they are interested in being better leaders. They know they haven't got it all figured out yet. They seek out new knowledge and new ways of doing stuff, especially the people stuff. They love hearing other people's experiences and insights. They crave growth and love a laugh. The leaders I work with come from diverse sectors, from agriculture, construction, higher education, retail, hospitality, social services, local, state, and federal government. If this sounds like a posse you'd love to be 'pod' of, check it out at www.zoerouth.com. We have various group programs that may suit you. Some are face-to-face and some are virtual, so you can attend from anywhere. You may be ready for a pod. If so, awesome! Likely you are also ready for more inspiring articles and podcasts – if so, go to www.zoerouth.com and sign up for my weekly podcasts.

For leaders who want to bring people stuff mastery to their broader organisation, let's chat. I work with a very small number of organisations each year. It's an exclusive and deep relationship where we fine-tune people stuff mastery and implement People First culture plans, which are unique to each organisation. The engagement begins with the leader, and I am very selective about who I choose to work with. I need to believe in you, the leader, and your commitment. Our values need to align. And we need to have fun!

That was my invitation to play.

In the meantime, live well, lead well.

Zoë Routh

June 2020

Q & A

Real life questions and answers from leaders and readers

Managing Up

Q1: "How do I give feedback to the executive team when they are exhibiting signs of the Four Devils?"

Channel your inner Elder to assess the situation.

Be curious: what is triggering their survival behaviour? Is it threats to power? Position? Place? Productivity?

Be compassionate: When have you not been the best version of yourself? What caused the poor behaviour? Could something similar be driving their behaviour?

Be wise: What are the systems or pressures in the organisation that might cause such poor behaviour? What are the consequences of raising the issues? What are the consequences if nothing is said? Which one are you prepared to accept?

Be courageous: if sharing insights is the option you choose, ask if one of them is open to a conversation about systems, processes, and effects. Share your perspective and explore together.

Q2: "How can I get people more senior than me to develop their people skills?"

The subtext of this question is that the senior leaders do not have adequate people skills. This is entirely possible. They could also be stuck in an organisational system that drives particular management behaviour. See the steps above to address this one.

One thing you might also consider is offering resources:

You might suggest, "Isaac, I've discovered some really useful resources that have helped me enormously in interacting with people. I'd love to get your perspective and insight."

or

"Have you read this book or listened to that podcast? I'd really value your point of view on this topic. I think we might be able to implement some of the ideas."

When we ask for advice from someone, they are immediately flattered and tend to look on us more favourably. When you frame a suggestion as a request for input, it highlights a learning and growth opportunity – for both of you. It's not just a 'you need to fix this' conversation.

Q3: "How do I manage up politically, sensitively, without too much detail but just enough?"

Again, there is loads of subtext here! "Without too much detail but just enough" speaks volumes to problems in the management structure, rather than the people.

Start with understanding what the threats are for the people involved. Are they likely to devolve into one of the Four Devils? How might you mitigate the threats in your messaging?

The fear of not wanting to share too much detail suggests there is concern that the receiver (s) of information will be interested if not alarmed by the detail and then wish to lean into more of the story. This might be solved from a system's point of view: clear articulation of responsibilities and boundaries, clear tracking of key performance indicators that are lead indicators rather than lag measures. It sounds a little like their trust is lacking. All trust issues need to be resolved from a system's point of view, not a personality one.

Next, it's time to channel your Diplomat. Be detached emotionally from the outcome. This is about a process of information sharing that is beneficial to the organisation's purpose. Maintain the Diplomat win-win stance: this is not about winning in spite of the senior leadership, but with them.

Q4: "How do I keep myself safe (from failing/compromising/ diminishing my future prospects) in an organisation with weak leadership?"

This is a Big Question. There is a lot at stake to stay or leave an organisation. We may not have the luxury of choice. There are many reasons why we may not be able to leave an organisation easily: fiscal responsibilities to extended family members, remote location where we have care for others and relocation would threaten their well-being.

So, if we do not have a safe choice to leave, then how do we stay?

What is 'weak leadership'? It might be that one or more of the executive are demonstrating one of the Four Devils. It might be that they are ill-equipped to deal with the current context, due to limited experience, or insufficient leadership maturity. In all cases, leaders who are 'weak' are deserving of compassion. It is a harrowing thing to find oneself in a leadership role and unprepared for its scope of responsibilities. It's a long fall from the top.

Having said that, we might consider positioning ourselves as 'wise counsel' or 'sage advisor' or even 'helpful resource' to the leaders. See the steps listed above in the previous questions.

If there does not appear to be any options for engaging or encouraging the leadership, start with where we are. Can we take actions within our own work environment to improve systems, communication and interactions? Can we be a leading light in a sea of grey? The organisation might have weak leadership, but parts of it, the parts that we manage, could be strong. Focus on that.

Q5: "How do I get agenda-driven managers to see the light of day?

This is a statement loaded with judgment. It's one of the shadow traps of the Elder: hubris and arrogance. In this question are two major judgments: the managers are 'agenda-driven' and they need 'to see the light of day' – presumably held by the enlightened question-asker.

If we are going to avoid devolving into the Elder's shadow of Tyrant, we need to check the arrogance and turn instead to curiosity, humility, and care as our guiding filters.

Humility: What am I not seeing? What are they trying to achieve that I am not yet aware of?

Curiosity: What is driving their need to drive an agenda? What is it about our systems that is creating this kind of unilateral obsession?

Care: What are they fearful of? What are the triggers that are keeping them blinkered?

By exploring the landscape from the perspective of the managers, we see where there might be opportunities to explore solutions, together.

Motivation

Q6: *"How do you manage a direct report that just doesn't want to be there?"*

It looks like a personality problem on the surface. All people stuff does.

We can start by looking at the map of motivators and demotivators.

Does their role have some intrinsic motivators? Do they have purpose? Opportunity for mastery? Autonomy to make decisions within a scoped framework?

Extrinsic motivators: do they get enough recognition? Appreciation? Is there a sense of belonging? Do they feel part of the team? Are they included in work and social activities?

Then look at the systems and environments: are the systems they engage with full of friction or allow for flow? Is there anything in their personal world that is draining heir internal resources? Things like a sick family member, a difficult marriage, an ailing dependent family member? Financial stresses?

When we look at the whole person, all of their triggers, and the systems that might be supporting or hindering them, then we have a chance to see if there is anything we can do or whether they need to choose somewhere else to go.

Q7: "How do you motivate people who are just intrinsically unmotivated?"

All people are motivated to do something, even if that something looks like nothing to us. When it comes to being unmotivated in our eyes, there are a number of causes. Let's look at these first before we look to solutions.

Structure of the environment

Delayed Reward. Reward has a big part to play in motivation. Sometimes when we have a big project or business, it can feel like the rewards are delayed far into the future. Given that our society and our culture is hardwired for immediate gratification, it's hard to sustain motivation over a long period of time without the dopamine hit of a quick win.

Unseen Payoff. It seems that we are toiling endlessly and that there is no win in sight. We don't know where the finish line is. We lack a sense of destination.

Unrealistic Goals. We might have set our sights on growing the business by 50% in one year. Instead of inspiring us, it's like a dead albatross around our neck.

Overwhelming Task. The task itself may seem overwhelming. It is very big and complex, and getting started feels like putting your shoulder against a massive boulder.

Perception issues

Here we see some of the triggers for the Four Devils.

Perception of power. Feeling demotivated can come from a loss of autonomy; the sense that decisions are being made to us instead of by us. That can bring about a sense of resignation and hopelessness.

Uncertainty. Not sure how the outcome will come about, what the results will be, or what our place is in the future. Cue deflation, like a saggy balloon.

Sense of self efficacy. We may feel like we don't have much power in the world in general. We may not believe that we have much talent either. Therefore, we feel that the big task ahead of us is simply not achievable for us, because we don't believe in ourselves.

How then to motivate the unmotivated:

1. Design the work environment with task in mind. Make tasks more defined and more achievable.
2. Design the environment to have enticing rewards that are meaningful to each person.
3. Give a sense of autonomy back to the team and individuals.
4. Reframe self-perception. Spend time developing influence skills, leadership skills, and strategic thinking skills.

Fundamentals

Q8: "How do you find people's drivers?"

Here we can use the people stuff maps we showcased in the Them chapter. Look at the balance of biochemicals in a person's experience.

How much are the tasks and experiences delivering opportunities for dopamine, oxytocin, serotonin, endorphins, and even cortisol? (A little stress, positively framed, can create excitement instead of worry).

Next, make sure the other triggers for the Four Devils are being managed:

Place – do they have a strong sense of belonging?

Power – do they have a sense of autonomy?

Position – are they being recognised? How do they like to be recognised?

Performance – are they progressing in their work?

By managing the biochemicals and the systems that support or impede them, you will have a really strong handle on drivers.

Q9: "What's the number one starting point for managing the people bit? Where would you start?"

Show them you see, hear, and value them. All of us want to feel valued and appreciated. Spark oxytocin with a kind smile and an encouraging nod as we listen to someone else's perspective.

Weird Stuff

These unusual and extreme people stuff problems are outside my explicit expertise, so I recommend getting clinical and legal advice. I also suggest listening to the great podcast interview I did with Certified Professional Behavior Analyst, Kerry Goyette[23].

Q10: How do you deal with a psychopath?

A psychopath is someone with a strong mental disorder with violent or antisocial tendencies. Absolutely we need to address behaviour that is threatening. Get legal and clinical support if required. We can also do this with compassion. Do some perspective taking – everyone has a history and a story. Mental disorders are not chosen conditions.

Q11: How do you deal with narcissists?

First, a narcissist is someone who lacks empathy for others and has an inflated sense of their own self importance. Their primary concern is for themselves.

Successful narcissists in the workplace are very smart and can be great individual contributors. Because of this they are hard to spot when they are not in leadership positions. It's only when they are in a group context that we might see how their behaviour shows selfish tendencies.

---

23 See zoerouth.com on the podcast page for the Kerry Goyette interview.

With any high potential leaders, we want to see them extend themselves, and even experience some failure. Of course we need to ensure we have created a 'safe to experiment and fail' work culture first! How people process and experience failure is a great indicator of self awareness and willingness to grow. If they default to blame shifting, they may exhibit signs of narcissism. In any case, blame shifting is not an attribute we want in our leaders!

If we suspect one of our team members is a narcissist, we can view them with compassion. They too have a perspective, often a really rough past, that has led to their self-absorbed outlook. Yet we need to be sensible as well as sensitive. If they are a peer, distance yourself from them socially. If they are a direct report, be aware of appointing them to leadership roles!

RESOURCES FOR LEADERS

Bibliography

Beck, D., and Gowan, C., 2005. *Spiral Dynamics: Mastering values, leadership, and change.* Malden: Blackwell; Reprint edition.

Bloom, P., 2016. *Against Empathy – The Case for Rational Compassion.* London: Bodley Head.

Breuning, L.G., 2016. *Habits of a Happy Brain: Retrain Your Brain To Boost Your Serotonin, Dopamine, Oxytocin & Endorphin levels.* Avon, Massachusetts: Adams Media.

Brown, B., 2005. *Rising Strong.* London: Vermilion.

Campbell, J., 2008. *The Hero with a Thousand Faces (The Collected Works of Joseph Campbell).* 3rd edition. Novato: New World Library.

Church, M., Stein, S., and Henderson, M., 2011. *Thought Leaders: How to capture, package, and deliver your ideas for greater commercial success.* Auckland: HarperCollins Publishers.

Damiano, S., 2014. *Leadership is Upside Down: The i4 Neuroleadership Revolution.* Neutral Bay Junction: About My Brain.

Ford, D., 2002. *The Secret of the Shadow: The Power of Owning Your Whole Story.* New York: HarperCollins.

Fosslien, L., West Duffy, M., 2019. *No Hard Feelings- The Secret Power of Harnessing Emotions At Work.* New York: Penguin Random House.

Frankl, V., 1959 (2004). *Man's Search for Meaning.* London: Rider, Ebury Publishing.

Gladwell, M., 2005. *Blink – The Power of Thinking Without Thinking.* London, Penguin.

Goleman D., 2006. *Social Intelligence: The New Science of Human Relationships.* New York: Hutchinson. pp 68-72

Goyette, K., 2019. *The Non Obvious Guide to Emotional Intelligence (You can actually use).* USA: The Idea Press.

Kahneman, D., 2011. *Thinking, Fast and Slow.* London, Penguin.

Keltner, D., 2016. *The Power Paradox: How We Gain and Lose Influence.* USA: Penguin Random House.

Murdock, M., 1998. *The Heroine's Journey: Woman's Quest for Wholeness.* Boston: Shambhala.

Nye, J., 2005. *Soft Power – The Means to Success in World Politics.* New York: Public Affairs, first edition.

Pearson, C., 1991. *Awakening the Heroes Within: Twelve Archetypes to Help Us Find Ourselves and Transform Our World.* 1st edition. New York: HarperCollins.

Pink, D., 2009. *Drive – The surprising truth about what motivates us.* Edinburgh: Canongate.

Robinson, M., 2012. *Everyone Matters: A Memoir.* London: Hodder & Stoughton.

Robson, D., 2019. *The Intelligence Trap: Why Smart People Make Stupid Mistakes – and How to Make Wiser Decisions.* London: Hodder & Stoughton.

Rock, D., 2009. *Your Brain At Work: Strategies for overcoming distraction, regaining focus, and working smarter all day long.* Pymble, Australia: HarperCollins.

Routh, Z., 2015. *Composure – How centered leaders make the biggest impact.* Canberra: Inner Compass Australia Pty Ltd.

Routh, Z., 2016. *Moments – Leadership when it matters most.* Canberra: Inner Compass Australia Pty Ltd.

Routh, Z., 2018. *Loyalty – Stop unwanted staff turnover, boost engagement, and create lifelong advocates.* Canberra: Inner Compass Australia Pty Ltd.

Torbert, B. and associates, 2004. *Action Inquiry: The Secret of Timely and Transforming Leadership.* San Francisco: Berrett-Koehler Publishers, Inc.

Trimboli, Oscar. 2017. *Deep Listening – Impact Beyond Words.* Sydney: www.oscartrimboli.com.

Walker, B. and Salt, D. 2012. *Resilience Practice: Building Capacity to Absorb Disturbance and Maintain Function.* Washington: Island Press.

White, F., 2018. *The Cosma Hypothesis: Implications of the Overview Effect.* Self published.

Wigglesworth, C., 2014. *SQ 21: The Twenty-One Skills of Spiritual Intelligence.* New York: Select Books.

Wilber, K., 2011. *The Essential Ken Wilber: An Introductory Reader.* Kindle edition. Boston: Shambhala.

Willinck, J., 2015, updated 2018. *Extreme Ownership: How U.S. Navy SEALS Lead and Win.* Sydney: Pan Macmillan Australia.

Articles

Sherman, G., 2019. "You don't bring bad news to the cult leader": Inside the fall of WeWork. *Vanity Fair.* Retrieved from https://www.vanityfair.com/news/2019/11/inside-the-fall-of-wework

Rothsteing, M., 2017. How Will WeWork Earn its $20B Valuation? Elementary School. *BISNOW.* Retrieved from https://www.bisnow.com/new-york/news/office/wework-school-wegrow-young-entrepreneurs-81203

Podcast Interviews

I interviewed some amazing leaders and experts in the research for this book on my podcast, aptly named, The *Zoë Routh Leadership Podcast*. Some are specifically mentioned in *People Stuff*, or ones that

I think are well worth listening to, include the ones listed below. Visit zoerouth.com/podcast-news to search for the ones you wish to listen to.

E152 – How to get your team to operate at full potential with Kerry Goyette

E146 – Uncertainty in Coronavirus: Create a new normal with Barry Pogorel

E145 – Coronavirus: Make a decision today, change it later – with CEO Toni Pergolin

E142 – Secrets to bad culture exposed – with Chris Dyer

E137 – How to be a Strategic Thinker – with Jo Metcalfe

E136 – How to Create Accountability in Direct Reports – with Corrinne Armour

E135 – Culture is everything – reward behaviour AND results – with CEO Craig Dower

E134 – My biggest failure was needing to be right – Marene Allison, CISO Johnson & Johnson

E131 – Be better – Don't hide from it, tackle it! With business owner Rob Evans

E129 – Stop rewarding outputs! Culture tips with bestselling author Josh Levine

E128 – Stop talking about diversity, start talking about SYMPHONY – Oshoke Pamela Abalu

E126 – How to be wise, compassionate and peaceful – Cindy Wigglesworth

E125 – Are you a smart person who makes dumb mistakes? With author David Robson

E122 – You don't need permission to create positive work experiences – with Shawn Murphy

E119 – 7 Values of Metamodern Leadership we need now – with James Surwillo

E118 – Diversity is difference, and difference is an asset – with Christina Ryan

E115 – One company, no B.S. – insights from Atlassian Team Coach Bernie Ferguson

E114 – We're all the same and a little bit different – Yenn Purkis, speaker author, Autism advocate, non binary gender person

E113 – Diversity and inclusion – How we do it at GHD, interview with Rory Waddell

GRATITUDE AND ACKNOWLEDGMENTS

There is so much wisdom in people's experiences! I want to thank all those who completed the survey I conducted. In particular I want to thank these leaders who made time for me to speak with me about their people stuff challenges: Cathy Phelps, Andrew Rice, Kathryn Adams, Ingrid Costello, Richard Dickmann, Michael Smith, Jason Strong, Elizabeth Brennan, Edwina Hayes.

Thanks goes to my team who have always believed in me and supported our work: Bianca Jurd, Krystal Rochford, Abby Lastimosa, and Louise Dalglish Smith.

Thanks also to my village of producers: Rebecca Stewart my trusty editor who backed this book from the start and helped me pull the threads together in a meaningful way; Eric Hook at Bookbound for taking it all and putting it into something tangible; and the amazing Lynne Cazaly who has brought it to life with the cover design and illustrations. I have never been more excited about a font!

To my own posse pod, my Thought Leader mates, thanks for being a safe place to be all of who I am, for sharing a rant and a laugh. Our friendship is treasured.

To my husband Rob for keeping me grounded and helping me to not take myself too seriously. I cherish this perspective.

To Steven Kotler, Brent Hogarth, Heidi Williams and the team at Flow Research Collective, thanks for the inspiration and re-kindling of my passion for writing as a special craft. The Flow for Writers course has brought focus and new purpose to my work. And now a new posse of writers to hang out with!

And to my clients: thank you for bringing me into your world, sharing your challenges and triumphs. You continue to inspire me and uplift me, knowing you are doing such great work in the world.

Zoë Routh

ABOUT THE AUTHOR

Zoë Routh is a leadership expert specialising in people stuff. She shows leaders and teams struggling with office politics and silos how to work better together.

She has worked with individuals and teams internationally and in Australia since 1987. From the wild rivers of northern Ontario to the remote regions of Australia, Zoë has spent the last 30 years or so showing teams how to navigate the wilderness of people stuff.

Zoë is the author of three previous books: *Composure – How centered leaders make the biggest impact* (2015), *Moments – Leadership when it matters most* (2016) and *Loyalty – Stop unwanted stuff turnover, boost engagement, and build lifelong advocates* (2018).

Her past leadership roles include Training Director at Outward Bound Australia, Chair of the Outdoor Council of Australia, President of the Chamber of Women in Business, and Program Manager at the Australian Rural Leadership Foundation.

Zoë is also the producer of the *Zoë Routh Leadership Podcast*, which is dedicated to exploring perspective in people stuff so we can live and lead better.

Zoë is an outdoor adventurist and enjoys telemark skiing, has run 6 marathons, is a one-time belly-dancer, has survived cancer, and loves hiking in the high country. She is married to a gorgeous Aussie and is mother to one remaining geriatric chook.

www.zoerouth.com

www.facebook.com/zoe.routh

twitter.com/zoerouth

au.linkedin.com/in/zoerouth

www.instagram.com/zoerouth/

APPENDICES

Appendix A: Trust in public life

Ketchell, M. (2018, December 5). Australians' trust in politicians and democracy hits an all-time low: new research. Retrieved from https://theconversation.com/australians-trust-in-politicians-and-democracy-hits-an-all-time-low-new-research-108161

"Just 31% of the population trust federal government. State and local governments perform little better, with just over a third of people trusting them. Ministers and MPs (whether federal or state) rate at just 21%, while more than 60% of Australians believe the honesty and integrity of politicians is very low.

The three biggest grievances people have with politicians are:

- They are not accountable for broken promises
- They don't deal with the issues that really matter
- Big business has too much power (Liberal and National Party voters identify trade unions instead of big business).

The continued decline of political trust has also contaminated public confidence in other key political institutions. Only five rate above 50% – police, military, civic well-being organisations (such as Headspace or community services), universities and healthcare institutions.

Trust was lowest in political parties (16%) and web-based media (20%). Trust in banks and web-based media has significantly decreased since the last survey. This reflects the impact of the banking royal commission and the Facebook-Cambridge Analytica data scandal."

Hanrahan, Catherine. (27 Nov 2019) Australia Talks: The most and least trusted professions revealed. Retrieved from https://www.abc.net.au/news/2019-11-27/the-professions-australians-trust-the-most/11725448

"Celebrities are trusted by just 8 per cent of Australians. Doctors and nurses, on the other hand, top the list, trusted by 97 per cent of us.

Scientists were the second-most trusted group (93 per cent), followed by police and law enforcement (84 per cent)."

Workplace Bullying and Violence, Safe Work Australia, retrieved from https://www.safeworkaustralia.gov.au/doc/infographic-workplace-bullying-and-violence

- One in three women who claim for a mental disorder stated it involved harassment or bullying
- One in five men who claim for a mental disorder stated it involved harassment or bullying
- Workers who report being sworn or yelled at in the workplace: 37%
- Workers who experienced unfair treatment due to gender: 11%
- Almost 20% of workers say they have experienced discomfort due to sexual humour
- Workers who report being physically assaulted or threatened by patients or clients: 22%
- Mental disorder claims that are caused by harassment, bullying or exposure to violence: 39%
- Mental stress claims as a result from exposure to occupational violence: 15%
- Mental stress claims made by workers aged 20-27 years were from exposure to workplace violence: 26%
- Mental stress claims made by workers under 20 years were from exposure to workplace violence: 31%

Appendix B: Famous thoughts on wisdom, compassion and perspective

Thoughts on wisdom

"By three methods we may learn wisdom: First, by reflection, which is noblest; Second, by imitation, which is easiest; and third by experience, which is the bitterest."
– Confucius

"The saddest aspect of life right now is that science gathers knowledge faster than society gathers wisdom."
– Isaac Asimov

"It is the mark of an educated mind to be able to entertain a thought without accepting it."
– Aristotle, *Metaphysics*

"Any fool can know. The point is to understand."
– Albert Einstein

"The unexamined life is not worth living."
– Socrates

"The more I read, the more I acquire, the more certain I am that I know nothing."
– Voltaire

"The desire to reach for the stars is ambitious. The desire to reach hearts is wise."
– Maya Angelou

"We shall not cease from exploration
And the end of all our exploring
Will be to arrive where we started
And know the place for the first time."
– T. S. Eliot, *Four Quartets*

"Wonder is the beginning of wisdom."
– Socrates

"It is one thing to be clever and another to be wise."
– George R.R. Martin

"Wisdom is not a product of schooling but of the lifelong attempt to acquire it."
– Albert Einstein

"A wise man gets more use from his enemies than a fool from his friends."
– Baltasar Gracian, *The Art of Worldly Wisdom*

"Simple can be harder than complex: You have to work hard to get your thinking clean to make it simple. But it's worth it in the end because once you get there, you can move mountains."
– Steve Jobs

"Where wisdom reigns, there is no conflict between thinking and feeling."
– Carl Gustav Jung

"I have lived with several Zen masters -- all of them cats."
– Eckhart Tolle, *The Power of Now: A Guide to Spiritual Enlightenment*

"A great many people think they are thinking when they are merely rearranging their prejudices."
– William James

> *"The man of wisdom is never of two minds;*
> *the man of benevolence never worries;*
> *the man of courage is never afraid."*
> – Confucius

> *"Voici mon secret. Il est très simple: on ne voit bien qu'avec le cœur. L'essentiel est invisible pour les yeux."*
> – Antoine de Saint-Exupéry, *Le Petit Prince*

> *"Wisdom is the reward for surviving our own stupidity."*
> – Brian Rathbone, Regent

Thoughts on compassion

> *"Be kind, for everyone you meet is fighting a harder battle."*
> – Plato

> *"Love and compassion are necessities, not luxuries. Without them, humanity cannot survive."*
> – Dalai Lama XIV, *The Art of Happiness*

> *"Compassion hurts. When you feel connected to everything, you also feel responsible for everything. And you cannot turn away. Your destiny is bound with the destinies of others. You must either learn to carry the Universe or be crushed by it. You must grow strong enough to love the world, yet empty enough to sit down at the same table with its worst horrors."*
> – Andrew Boyd, *Daily Afflictions: The Agony of Being Connected to Everything in the Universe*

> *"Our task must be to free ourselves... by widening our circle of compassion to embrace all living creatures and the whole of nature and its beauty."*
> – Albert Einstein

> "If you want others to be happy, practice compassion.
> If you want to be happy, practice compassion."
> – Dalai Lama XIV, *The Art of Happiness*

> "Compassion is not a relationship between the healer and the wounded. It's a relationship between equals. Only when we know our own darkness well can we be present with the darkness of others. Compassion becomes real when we recognize our shared humanity."
> – Pema Chödrön, *The Places That Scare You: A Guide to Fearlessness in Difficult Times*

> "Until he extends the circle of his compassion to all living things, man will not himself find peace."
> – Albert Schweitzer

> "Men build too many walls and not enough bridges."
> – Joseph Fort Newton

> "Only the development of compassion and understanding for others can bring us the tranquility and happiness we all seek."
> – Dalai Lama XIV

> "Every single time you help somebody stand up you are helping humanity rise."
> – Steve Maraboli, *Life, the Truth, and Being Free*

Thoughts on perspective

> "If you're wondering what I mean by 'miracle', it's simple: a miracle is a shift in perspective from fear to love."
> – Gabrielle Bernstein

> "The greatest tragedy for any human being is going through their entire lives believing the only perspective that matters is their own."
> – Doug Baldwin

"The only thing you sometimes have control over is your perspective. You don't have control over your situation. But you have a choice about how you view it."
– Chris Pine

"Be willing to be a beginner every single morning."
– Meister Eckhart Tolle

"It's not what you look at that matters; it's what you see."
– Henry David Thoreau

"If you change the way you look at things, the things you look at change."
– Wayne Dyer

"Everything we hear is an opinion, not a fact. Everything we see is perspective, not the truth."
– Marcus Aurelius

"If you don't like something, change it. If you can't change it, change the way you think about it."
– Mary Engelbreit

"Persons appear to us according to the light we throw upon them from our own minds."
– Laura Ingalls Wilder

"Your reality is as you perceive it to be. So, it is true, that by altering our perception we can alter our reality."
– William Constantine

"Attachment constrains our vision so that we are not able to see things from a wider perspective."
– Dalai Lama

"There are no facts, only interpretations."
– Friedrich Nietzsche

"One person's craziness is another person's reality."
– Tim Burton

"The difference between hope and despair is a different way of telling stories from the same facts."
– Alain de Botton

"Your life is a print-out of your thoughts."
– Steve Maraboli, *Life, the Truth, and Being Free*

"Distance lends enchantment to the view."
– Mark Twain

"We begin to learn wisely when we're willing to see the world from other people's perspective."
– Toba Beta, *Master of Stupidity*

"The huge problems we deal with every day are actually really small. We're so focused on what bothers us that we don't even try to see our lives from a clearer perspective."
– Susane Colasanti, *Something Like Fate*

"Beauty is in the eye of a beholder.
No perspective, no perception.
New perspective, new perception."
– Toba Beta, *Master of Stupidity*

"Remember, you see in any situation what you expect to see."
– David Schwartz

www.ingramcontent.com/pod-product-compliance
Lightning Source LLC
Chambersburg PA
CBHW070424010526
44118CB00014B/1891